"Drawing on years of experience in [...] relationships built with the unhoused ~~people he has met~~ along the way, Kevin Nye skillfully walks readers through the complex issues that surround homelessness while casting a powerful theological vision that calls us to shelter all God's people through hope and faithful action. Personal and prophetic, practical and powerful, *Grace Can Lead Us Home* is desperately needed, breathing love and new life into a grace-filled response to the housing and homelessness crisis."

—**REV. DR. JACQUI LEWIS**, senior minister of Middle Collegiate Church and author of *Fierce Love: A Bold Path to Ferocious Courage and Rule-Breaking Kindness That Can Heal the World*

"By drawing readers back to the biblical vision of justice, Kevin Nye gives us a new lens for seeing our unhoused neighbors. He breaks open common myths about the causes of homelessness and challenges attitudes in the church that essentially blame people for their trauma. Instead, Nye articulates as well as lives out neighbor-love that is less about 'us and them' and more about 'we,' who are equally in need of grace. This vision isn't just about addressing homelessness but also about remembering our humanity."

—**KATELYN BEATY**, editor and author of *Celebrities for Jesus*

"I am so glad this book exists because as Christians we worship a homeless Savior yet when we encounter people experiencing homelessness, our response often lands somewhere between indifference and outright rejection. This is not the way of Jesus. In *Grace Can Lead Us Home*, Kevin Nye challenges us to rethink what it means to be the people of God in and for the world, particularly in how we practically go about loving and serving our neighbors in need. If your heart breaks every time you walk by someone sleeping on the sidewalk but you don't know how to be Christ to them, this is the book for you."

—**ZACK HUNT**, author of *Unraptured: How End Times Theology Gets It Wrong*

"My best friend's father was unhoused for years. She would visit him in a tent off the side of a highway. Kevin Nye will help you see that unhoused people are fathers, and mothers, and family members, and friends. They are human beings worthy of our attention and deserving of dignity. *Grace Can Lead Us Home* is a book about love, compassion, and the value of humanity."

—**HEATHER THOMPSON DAY**, author of *It's Not Your Turn*

"In *Grace Can Lead Us Home*, Kevin Nye partakes in the sacred work of rehumanization. In illustrating some realities of our neighbors experiencing homelessness, he shows us where we might find Jesus. In showing us how we might overcome this reality, he shows us how we might embody Jesus."

—**R. G. A. "TREY" FERGUSON III**, founding president of RFX Ministries, director of equipping at Refuge Church Miami, and cohost of *Three Black Men* podcast

"This timely, moving, well-researched book is an exploration of the stunning injustice of mass homelessness in one of the wealthiest countries in the world. What is so astounding is not only that so much human suffering exists, but that we— Christians—have allowed it to endure for so long. These pages contain a call to compassion, community, and justice. They implore us to reexamine our preconceived notions and to transform our hearts, minds, and world."

—**LINDSEY KRINKS**, author of *Praying with Our Feet*

"In exploring the grace of perhaps the most famous person in history to experience homelessness, Jesus Christ, Kevin Nye reveals the Christ in the millions of people experiencing homelessness in the world today. In doing so, Nye follows the call of God by proposing a bold but necessary plea: to end homelessness."

—**MASON MENNENGA**, YouTuber and host of *A People's Theology* podcast

GRACE
CAN LEAD US
HOME

A
CHRISTIAN
CALL TO END
HOMELESSNESS

KEVIN NYE

HERALD
P R E S S

Harrisonburg, Virginia

Herald Press
PO Box 866, Harrisonburg, Virginia 22803
www.HeraldPress.com

Library of Congress Cataloging-in-Publication Data
Names: Nye, Kevin, author.
Title: Grace can lead us home : a Christian call to end homelessness / Kevin Nye.
Description: Harrisonburg, Virginia : Herald Press, 2022. | Includes bibliograph-
   ical references.
Identifiers: LCCN 2022010441 (print) | LCCN 2022010442 (ebook) | ISBN
   9781513810515 (paper) | ISBN 9781513810522 (h/c) | ISBN
   9781513809823 (audiobook) | ISBN 9781513810539 (ebook)
Subjects: LCSH: Church work with the homeless. | Homelessness—Religious
   aspects—Christianity. | BISAC: RELIGION / Christian Living / Social Issues
   | SOCIAL SCIENCE / Social Classes & Economic Disparity
Classification: LCC BV4456 .N94 2022 (print) | LCC BV4456 (ebook) | DDC
   261.8/325—dc23/eng/20220318
LC record available at https://lccn.loc.gov/2022010441
LC ebook record available at https://lccn.loc.gov/2022010442

Study guides are available for many Herald Press titles at www.HeraldPress.com.

GRACE CAN LEAD US HOME
© 2022 by Kevin Nye. Released by Herald Press, Harrisonburg, Virginia 22803.
   800-245-7894. All rights reserved.
Library of Congress Control Number: 2022010441
International Standard Book Number: 978-1-5138-1051-5 (paperback);
   978-1-5138-1052-2 (hardcover); 978-1-5138-1053-9 (ebook);
   978-1-5138-0982-3 (audiobook)
Printed in United States of America
Cover and interior design by Merrill Miller

   Unless otherwise noted, scripture text is quoted, with permission, from the
New Revised Standard Version Bible, copyright © 1989, Division of Christian
Education of the National Council of the Churches of Christ in the United States
of America. Used by permission. All rights reserved.
   Scripture quotations marked NIV are taken from the *Holy Bible, New
International Version*®, NIV®. Copyright © 1973, 1978, 1984, 2011 by Biblica,
Inc.® Used by permission of Zondervan. All rights reserved worldwide. www
.zondervan.com The "NIV" and "New International Version" are trademarks reg-
istered in the United States Patent and Trademark Office by Biblica, Inc.®

26 25 24 23 22   10 9 8 7 6 5 4 3 2 1

For Naomi,
my partner in joy and (mis)adventure

CONTENTS

FOREWORD

ONE OF THE greatest threats to persons experiencing home-lessness is not only exclusion, lack of access to resources, and the constant fight to belong, but also the narratives that fuel the criminalization, mistreatment, and lens through which this population is constantly seen. Narrative is powerful because narrative can empower, liberate, and humanize, and it can affirm the inherent worth and value that all persons carry, regardless of whether they have an address.

However, narrative in the wrong hands can limit, dehu-manize, exclude, and create social frames that can provoke per-sons to otherize those who are vulnerable. When it comes to people experiencing homelessness, we must provide the type of narrative justice for those who are without homes in such a way that they are included and experience the same type of belonging that we all want for ourselves.

When I mention narrative justice, I define it along the lines of a recent Twitter thread of mine: "Narrative justice as it relates to homelessness is about correcting the false narratives that continue to fuel the mistreatment and criminalization of those without an address. . . . Narrative justice is about letting those who have been silenced by exclusion have access to a microphone that has been dominated by the voices of people who have never experienced homelessness or shared their power with people on the margins."[1]

Kevin Nye's book is about this very concept—calling us to extend to others the grace of God that we so freely want for ourselves. This book calls us to share the love of God with a community that is often invisible to our larger society, and it calls us to rewrite the narratives that surround those without homes. Jesus himself said that he came to earth to share good news with those who are poor and have been oppressed by systems of injustice, and he calls us in a similar manner to show up for our neighbors without homes.

No longer can we sit back and allow belonging to serve only a select few; no longer can we allow those who experience homelessness to be defined in ways that go against the very dignity that every single person possesses. No longer can we allow ignorance about the subject of homelessness to cause us to build walls instead of extending longer tables that have grace at the center.

Good news is for everyone. It is for the person living behind a building. It is for the teenager who has been disowned because that teen identifies a certain way. It is for the family that has been evicted, and for those who are living out of their car while also working a job that doesn't pay a living wage. It is for the person who is newly experiencing the plight of homelessness because of the loss and grief of COVID-19. This work is for anyone who hasn't found a "home," both physically and sociologically.

Nye's book calls us to rethink how Christians who carry the love of God show up for those who are experiencing homelessness, criminalization, and displacement. He calls us to reflect on the words that Jesus uttered: "Foxes have holes, and birds of the air have nests; but the Son of Man has nowhere to lay his head" (Matthew 8:20).

After I met Kevin Nye, I felt compelled to support his work because he has a heart to lend his voice to those who have been silenced; his work is honest, vulnerable, and committed to using both pain and privilege to educate those willing to listen.

Nye calls us to reflect on the fact that Jesus knows what it means to be displaced, and understands the experience of not having a place to lay his head; yet Jesus still shows up to extend the grace of God to all who are weary and experiencing marginalization and spiritual impoverishment. That's good news!

This book is for any Christian who has a heart to join the fight in caring and advocating for a group of people who are invisible or othered in our society and desperately in need of having their dignity affirmed. This book is for every person who needs to be reminded that the table of grace also extends to those who do not have a roof.

—Terence Lester, founder of Love Beyond Walls
and author of *I See You: How Love Opens Our Eyes
to Invisible People* and *When We Stand: The Power
of Seeking Justice Together*

A NOTE ON LANGUAGE

THROUGHOUT THIS BOOK, you will notice that I almost never use the word *homeless* on its own, unless it appears in a quote or functions in the official name of a service provider. The term is falling out of use in favor of a few different terms that more helpfully frame the issue. When we hear the phrase "homeless person," our minds immediately conjure a fairly stereotypical image: usually an adult man with unkempt hair wearing soiled clothes and pushing a shopping cart or holding a cardboard sign. But statistics indicate that homelessness is much broader than this—in fact, the average age of a "homeless person" in America is eleven years old,[1] and a person is more likely to stay overnight in a shelter as an infant than at any other age.[2]

Most often I use the phrase *person* (or *people*) *experiencing homelessness*. This "person first" language emphasizes humanity and personhood first, before an individual's state of homelessness. Describing homelessness as an "experience" has the added benefit of connoting its temporariness. When we say "homeless person," the adjective *homeless* occupies the position of traits that are normally associated with intrinsic, permanent characteristics such as skin color (e.g., a lighter-skinned person or a darker-skinned person).

I also use the term *unhoused person* (or *people*). While this phrasing doesn't use person-first language, it helpfully focuses the issue on housing, which is a more tangible, political reality than something as loosely definable as "home." Additionally, *housed* functions as an adjectival form of the verb *to house*. Implied in this linguistic structure is not simply that people are without housing, but that no one has housed them. This phrasing recognizes the responsibility a community has in ensuring that people have access to housing, rather than presenting it solely as something a person lacks.

With that said, I have rarely encountered a person experiencing homelessness who has a strong opinion on the terminology used to describe them. In fact, they are the ones whom I most often hear using the "outdated" terminology. One person I knew put it bluntly: "I don't care what you call us, what are you going to do to help us?" This is a helpful reminder that changing our language to be more open, accurate, and compassionate toward people is no replacement for actually acting for good on their behalf. Nonetheless, I do believe in shifting our language toward the options listed above; though it may not do a lot to directly serve or dignify the person to or about whom we're speaking, I do believe it changes *me*. When we cultivate better language, our imaginations and our actions can follow suit. For this reason, I will use *experiencing homelessness* and *unhoused* interchangeably throughout these pages.

INTRODUCTION

WHEN I CHOSE to give up a future in traditional church ministry in 2018, I was already several years into a career in homelessness services, working for a nonreligious nonprofit in Hollywood called The Center. Despite having received a master of divinity from Fuller Seminary and almost completing the process of ordination in the Church of the Nazarene, my widening sense of call and vocation wasn't matching the traditional "pastoral" trajectory.

Shortly after my decision, the denomination's Los Angeles District held its annual assembly, at which pastors and church members gather for several days to vote on a few denominational matters and worship together. During the Thursday evening ceremony, candidates who have successfully completed the ordination process are confirmed as ministers in the denomination. Wanting to express my commitment and gratitude to the denomination despite my decision not to pursue ordination, I chose to attend. I knew it would be hard to sit through the ceremony as an observer when I could have been standing onstage, but I still wanted to participate in the denominational community.

Withdrawing from ordination had been an extremely vulnerable and personal process, one that included letting down a number of friends and family members who couldn't understand how a career in homelessness services might fulfill a calling to Christian ministry. Working among and advocating for people experiencing homelessness felt like a calling, and certainly felt like "ministry." At the same time, many people in positions of authority over me could not make that connection; time spent at work wouldn't be counted toward my ministry hours needed for ordination. In my heart, my call to ministry and this work were one and the same, but no matter how passionately I articulated it, many refused to see the connection.

During the ceremony, the two people who supported me most throughout the process, my wife Naomi and our pastor, sat on either side and comforted me with knowing glances and timely hands on my shoulders. We sat through about two-thirds of the service before leaving together.

As we reached the parking lot, a man approached us. I could immediately recognize that he was experiencing homelessness and some form of mental illness. Call it occupational awareness; I'm not always right, but you come to recognize the signs over time.

Most of my job, to that point, was talking to people—getting to know the names and stories of whoever walked into The Center off the streets. It was awkward, at first. I wondered what I would talk about. The weather? Might be a touchy subject for people who have to sleep in it. Seen any good movies lately? They're probably not catching the latest blockbuster at the theater like I am. But as my comfort improved, so did my skills, and I became better at engaging with people experiencing homelessness, better able to address their needs both as clients and as people.

And yet, even though talking to people experiencing homelessness had become my expertise, when this man made eye contact with me, I felt a familiar anxiety, discomfort, and even a bit of frustration; the same feelings that people who aren't service professionals tell me they feel when they have these encounters, the same feelings I used to feel. Part of it is boundaries—it's hard to do this for work every day and still encounter it in my time off. In another way, though, these interactions never become normal. Why should they? There's nothing natural about how commonly we encounter desperation in our cities, even for those of us who are on the frontlines of addressing it.[1]

When the man reached us, I used a lot of the tricks of the trade I'd learned along the way. First, I just listened; often enough, people simply want to be heard. My instincts about his mental health had been right: he spoke in a mix of paranoid delusion and quasi-religious symbolism with a dash of current events. I tried a technique called grounding, often used when someone's mental health symptoms are flaring. The goal is to bring the person's mind back into the present moment by increasing their awareness of their surroundings, especially specific buildings or landmarks, or more abstract things like colors or sounds. If you can guide the person back to themself, even just for a second, they might be able to more clearly express their wants or needs.

In this case, it seemed all he wanted from us was some human interaction. After a while, I used one last skill I had learned over time: gracefully stopping a conversation with people who are unable to stop themselves. He walked toward the church, and as we got to our cars I saw him open the door and go inside. I wondered whether he'd be asked to leave.

If there's one thing that unifies nearly every significant moment of my life, it's that I don't notice the significance until much, much later. As much as I've learned to ground others during conversations, it can be easy to lose my own awareness of the present moment and its significance. I had stepped out of a service that would have been *my* ordination, a milestone in a path that at one time had given my life great direction and purpose. Friends and family would have attended and celebrated with me. Instead, I found myself in the church parking lot, literally between the church and the streets, talking to a paranoid, isolated man who probably spent his days ignored or, at best, simply placated.

This experience signaled to me a place I would come to occupy, a place I believe God has put me—with one foot in that ordination service, called to serve and love the church, and one foot in the streets, where those whom the world has rejected sleep, suffer, and die. Whichever way I turn and face, one message continues to emerge: grace.

In my work at The Center, I bring to bear all that I've learned about who God is and whom God loves. Whether I'm helping move someone into an apartment or debating policy in a meeting with local officials, my church upbringing and theological education are ever present. Everything I have come to believe about God informs my advocacy for the unhoused.

The reverse has also been true, in that I have consistently found that my work in homelessness informs my theology: confirming beliefs about God's justice, challenging my role in God's work, and redefining and expanding my theological categories and ideas. It is precisely here that I see an opportunity to reflect back to the church what I have seen and learned. I believe and trust that the church is aching, as I was, to do something about homelessness; that when we see a person languishing on the streets, the love and compassion of God moves in us and wants to move through us. In these moments, though, we may feel that we as individuals or as churches are not equipped to tackle a problem that feels so complex and enormous.

This book aims to bridge that gap by reporting back the stories, experiences, and education I've received in my time learning from hundreds of men and women experiencing homelessness, many of whom I now consider friends. I want to tell you about Christ as I have met him most clearly—in tents, shelters, and drop-in centers. I believe he has something to teach us all about grace, a lesson that can come only from the margins. And I believe that lesson can teach us all we need to know to change the landscape of homelessness entirely.

I believe it can teach us how to end homelessness.

ᴺᴺᴺᴺᴺ

I'll never forget the night I first saw Skid Row. It was a total accident that I turned down Sixth Street looking for the highway, but what I saw would leave an indelible mark on my soul. People and belongings were strewn about with no discernible barrier between the sidewalk and the street. Individuals slumped against buildings looking half dead, and others darted restlessly around the unboundaried space.

I'd left Pershing Square—a beautiful park in the middle of Downtown Los Angeles, home to an ice-skating rink every winter, drawing families and couples from across the county—just minutes before. I had taken Naomi there on our first date, and we had decided to prolong our time together by finding a highway and seeing where it would take us. But one "wrong" turn took us immediately from an epicenter of smiling wealth into what a UN representative would describe that same year as comparable to a Syrian refugee camp.[2]

Skid Row is a historic neighborhood in Los Angeles and a longtime hub for folks who are poor and in transition. At the turn of the twentieth century, it was home to a thriving community of seasonal workers who would come by train to Downtown Los Angeles and live night to night in one of the dozens of single-room occupancy hotels that were designed to accommodate exactly that population. Eventually, though, revitalization projects knocked down most of these housing complexes, effectively demolishing LA's historic core of afford-able housing. When homelessness escalated in the 1980s, this neighborhood became the central gathering place for people experiencing homelessness, as well as the services and missions meant to help them.

From then on, Skid Row was unofficially designated as the only place one could sleep on the streets in LA. If you were found experiencing homelessness in any part of the county, you would find yourself in a police cruiser on a one-way trip to Skid Row. To this day, when someone is released from jail or prison with no place to go, they are put on a bus at two in the morning that drops them off in the middle of Skid Row. What was decades ago referred to as Hell's Half Acre now encom-passes fifty city blocks, nearly three square miles. I once heard local pastor Rev. Kelvin Sauls preach, "In the so-called City of Angels, Hell's Half Acre is expanding its territory. Hell is winning."

And he's right—after the 2008 recession, Skid Row could no longer contain the numbers of people experiencing homelessness, and encampments began to form all across the city. By the time I arrived in Los Angeles, I could hardly drive a block or two without coming across an encampment or a person in distress. Even today, homelessness is scattered across every corner of Los Angeles while still remaining especially concentrated and devastating in Skid Row, an abandoned community with little to hope for.

At this same time, I was attending seminary, and was drawn to the prophets of the exile, especially Jeremiah. The people of God were living in an unfamiliar land, disappointed that things hadn't quite worked out the way they'd hoped. The prophet instructs the people on how to build a new life within these circumstances. My favorite part is in chapter 29, verse 7, which reads, "But seek the welfare of the city where I have sent you into exile, and pray to the LORD on its behalf, for in its welfare you will find your welfare." Many people love and have memorized verse 11: "For surely I know the plans I have for you, says the LORD, plans for your welfare and not for harm, to give you a future with hope." The word *welfare*, used in both verses and translated from the Hebrew word *shalom*, which connotes holistic peace and completeness, clues us in to the larger message of the passage: the welfare that God has for us is not merely a general promise of happiness and fortune, but is instead directly tied to the welfare of everyone around us.

After that experience of accidentally driving through Skid Row with my future wife, it was clear that God's shalom was deeply needed in addressing homelessness. Los Angeles County, with around sixty thousand people experiencing homelessness, is responsible for 10 percent of the entire homeless population in the United States, with little overall change for about fifteen years. Like most compassionate, thoughtful Christians, I knew that *something* needed to be done, but I had no clue what. Regardless, I had to believe that God had something better for Los Angeles, and I wanted to join in that work.

ᗺᗺᗺᗺᗺ

Theologian John Wesley described grace as God's "bounty" and "free, undeserved favor." God freely offers us mercy and love in abundance not because we deserve it, not because of who we are, but because of who God is. This grace, demonstrated in the life, death, and resurrection of Jesus, is what invites us into communion with God and gives us the template for living together in a beloved community; it is the very foundation of our faith.

This grace occupies a very personal, intimate dimension—it is God's grace that wins us over despite our doubt, our belief that we are unworthy of love, belonging, and mercy. But God has declared that we are worthy; not on our own terms, but on God's. As an old pastor of mine said, "God has made up God's mind about you, and the news is good." And as this grace begins to take hold of us, it transforms us into people who begin to embody grace in every aspect of our lives. My denomination, and others that are founded on Wesley's teachings, call this *sanctifying grace*: "Through the power of the Holy Spirit we are enabled to increase in the knowledge and love of God and in love for our neighbor."[3] Grace, if allowed to take root in us, can change the way we see everything.

Grace is deeply personal to each one of us, but it also sweeps us up together in its grand movement. If a community of grace-shaped people turned toward their neighbors with the love and grace of God, how could the neighborhood itself help but be transformed? It is on this basis I believe that grace is key to ending homelessness.

The title of this book is based on a verse from that familiar hymn "Amazing Grace" by John Newton:

> *Through many dangers, toils, and snares*
> *I have already come;*
> *'tis grace that brought me safe thus far,*
> *and grace will lead me home.*

Ever since the first day of what is now my career in homelessness services, I hear the word *home* very differently. It can mean any number of things. Sometimes it is used synonymously with *house*, but it often connotes more—a feeling of safety or security associated with where you live. Christians sometimes refer to their place of worship as their "church home," again referring not only to the mere fact that they worship there but to how this place carries deep personal significance. Similarly, Christians look forward to a "heavenly home" after death that represents not just a physical destination but a spiritual, mystical culmination of all good things. As with grace, there is a breadth to the word *home* that goes beyond the literal.

When we talk about homelessness, we often don't bring this larger concept of home into the conversation. While literal housing and tangible resources are absolutely essential, we would do well to recognize that the experience of homelessness entails a disconnection from more than just physical resources; it is isolating, dehumanizing, and traumatizing. However crucial the role of housing in ending homelessness, we cannot forget that the experience of being *home*less also means a loss or lack of the many things we associate with "home," things as indispensable as safety, belonging, dignity, and hope.

A big reason we miss this is because we, as Christians, are prone to understanding homelessness in simple moral terms. A recent poll conducted by the *Washington Post* and Kaiser Research, aimed at discovering different groups' inherent beliefs about poverty, found that Christians are more than *twice* as likely as non-Christians to associate poverty with a lack of effort, as opposed to difficult circumstances.[4] This focus on individual failure versus systemic pressure implies that people experiencing homelessness "deserve" their plight, and that Christians are morally justified in letting them face the consequences of their own failure.

While I intend to interrogate these "Christian" beliefs about the causes of homelessness, it is crucial that we recognize the role that grace plays in undermining our calculations about what people deserve. If grace means that God gives us good things because of who God is, not because we deserve it, then who are we to base our approach to homelessness on whether those on the streets have earned or qualified for our help? If God's grace is enough for us, then it is enough for anyone experiencing homelessness, whether they are in that position because of moral failures, difficult circumstances, or any combination of reasons.

ᴻᴻᴻᴻᴻ

This book is an attempt to locate grace in our approach to homelessness. We will explore the practical social issues that are interrelated with homelessness: housing, mental illness, substance use, addiction, and more. In examining these issues, one of my primary objectives will be myth-busting. As it relates to poverty and homelessness, our beliefs are often shaped by prejudices and assumptions that are simply untrue and disprovable, thanks to decades of indispensable research and reporting. More than that, though, the beliefs we hold are often misaligned with our theology. We will come to see that there are better ways to see homelessness and all its facets that align not only with best practices, but also with God's vision of us, housed and unhoused, as neighbors.

Other chapters will delve into topics we don't normally consider when it comes to homelessness, such as isolation, flourishing, celebration, and abundance. As I've come to understand the crisis up close and from a theological and biblical perspective, these themes have emerged as overlooked yet crucial aspects of understanding and ending homelessness.

I will tell of my experiences alongside actual people whose lives and stories embody many of the ideas we will be exploring. All these stories are true to the best of my memory, and where possible, were fact-checked by others who were also present. Names have been changed where necessary to protect the privacy and dignity of the individuals about whom I'm writing. These stories will serve to remind us that these issues, which can often feel heady, intellectual, or philosophical, are about real people who, like all of us, have full lives that include suffering and pain but also joy and meaning.

My prayer is that this book is informative and leads to empathy and action. I pray that you will see things for the way they truly are; that you will understand why they are that way; that you'll be moved to lament and righteous anger for those who have to experience it; and that through it all you will be motivated to act because of the simple truth that things don't have to stay the way they are.

The pattern of grace invites us into this work: coming to us as an unexpected gift, forming and transforming us, sending us out and catching us up, together, in its work. None of us deserve the grace that God extends to us, yet it is extended all the same. For people experiencing homelessness, grace may feel far away, cut off by a world that sleeps better by believing that everyone is where they deserve to be. But grace tells a different story, and it sets the standard for what we all deserve as children of God.

If we embrace it, grace can lead us all home.

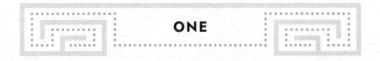

ONE

Seeing and Being Seen

I once was lost, but now I'm found,
was blind, but now I see.
—**JOHN NEWTON**, "Amazing Grace"

OUR LANGUAGE IS riddled with words of "seeing" that mean something more. When we elect leaders, we wonder about their "views" on particular topics, their "vision" for our communities, and their "outlook" on life and the human experience. How we "see" is ultimately about so much more than the light that enters our eyes and is interpreted by our brains. How we see isn't just what we look at, but how we look at it, and the world of values we project onto it.

Throughout Scripture, imagery of eyes, sight, and blindness is used to denote more than literal "seeing." It often signifies someone's ability to perceive God's truth, purpose, or values. In Matthew 6:22, Jesus puts a finer point on this by describing the eyes as "the lamp of the body," a curious metaphor, as we in our modern understanding know that our eyes receive light, but do not generate it. But for Jesus, the way that we "see" is so much more than what our eyes literally take in, and it has implications for our entire being.

As we look at homelessness in this book, the first invitation is to see differently. Having worked around homelessness in a few different contexts, the way I see homelessness has evolved and shifted dramatically over the years. From the first time I noticed a panhandler on the freeway off-ramp by my church to my most recent day at work, my perception of homelessness could not be more different. In the interplay between theology and Scripture and the experiences I've had in communion with the unhoused, I have come closer to seeing homelessness the way I think God does. In the process, I myself have been changed as my perception of my place in the story has been readjusted, and my assumptions about what we all deserve completely upended.

A new vision

As part of a scholarship-internship program I participated in through my theology and ministry major at Southern Nazarene University in Bethany, Oklahoma, I was to serve in a local church for an increasing number of hours each year, as I also received a scholarship that concurrently increased each year. My freshman and sophomore years were spent in the junior high ministry at one of the largest churches in our denomination, which boasted almost one hundred students in seventh and eighth grade alone. I had a lot of fun hanging out with middle schoolers for two years, but I was already starting to sense God's interruption of my plan to become a youth pastor and then eventually a senior pastor.

Penn Avenue Church was known around the department as "the homeless church." It was located on the outskirts of the Oklahoma City metro area near warehouses and overflowing thrift shops. It was pastored by a compassionate but reserved man who also ran a nonprofit called OKC Compassion out of the church building. This ministry was the real draw of the space, serving around sixty-five of Oklahoma City's unhoused every day with meals, Bible studies, clothing, and Celebrate Recovery meetings. The Sunday church service was populated by many of these same individuals, but also by a surprising number of salt-of-the-earth adults, including older adults, who saw what the church did with its compassionate ministry and decided that it warranted not only their support, but their dedication to the whole church.

Two nights before I was set to visit, I had a dream that I was interning at Penn Avenue/OKC Compassion. In the dream, an outdoor platform served as the church's stage, with many unkempt-looking folks milling about, drinking coffee, smoking, and making small talk. And I was simply there, observing, among them . . . and comfortable. I would come to find out a few days later this was not at all an accurate vision of the layout of the church. This was not a premonition or a "vision," but merely a concoction of my imagination plus the little I had heard. I thought almost nothing of it the next day, and then forgot about it for years.

If I'm honest, though, had it not been for the dream, I might've found a reason to skip on Sunday. Either way, I was probably going to ask for an extension to submit my desired church placement, and Saturday nights rarely lent themselves to responsible bedtimes when I was nineteen. On top of it all, Penn Avenue was an intimidating place to visit. I didn't know anyone, and the people I anticipated seeing there, "homeless people," weren't exactly people I knew how to relate to or strike up a conversation with. What if I didn't like it? Scarier still: What if I did?

The dream moved me ever so subtly from dismissal to reluctance, from a "probably not" to a "maybe?" Even though the Penn Avenue in my dream wasn't real or accurate, my hang-up was never about the church—it was about me. And somehow in the dream I felt strangely comfortable in that environment, among "those" people. I had to *see* it, though not in a literal sense, before I could believe it. The dream moved the needle just enough for me to actually go that Sunday, and to eventually experience that same level of comfort in the real Penn Avenue.

The real surprise of actually visiting the church that Sunday was how normal it was. At that point in my life, I had been to Sunday morning services at more than fifty churches, and Penn Avenue was shockingly ordinary. As a visitor, talking to strangers, visibly homeless or not, was just as weird that Sunday as it had been every other Sunday of my life. The music was fine, the preaching was good enough, and the people were nice—every single one of them. And I was comfortable enough in the setting to approach the pastor, express my interest, and ultimately be welcomed into that community for the next two years.

While I couldn't articulate it at the time, experiencing plain old church with the eclectic people of Penn Avenue was teaching me a new way to see the work I would one day call my vocation. Showing up for my hours often meant just coming during the mealtime and eating with the unhoused who had gathered. I developed two closer mentoring relationships at the behest of the pastor, which mainly meant spending extra time together, sometimes away from the church—I would take my "mentees" to McDonald's or Starbucks, or bring them up to my college campus to shoot pool in the cafe lounge.

While I would get a fuller picture of this later, I was learning to see the work of helping the unhoused differently. In those meals at the church and those coffee outings to McDonald's, I was learning that good work in homeless services is as much about the relationships and community you form as the services you render, or the perceived "progress" someone makes. So much holy and transformative work happens in the innocuous moments when people are simply together, sharing an experience, participating in an activity, and being humans in community.

Even after two years serving at Penn Avenue and OKC Compassion, there was much that I didn't yet see. In many ways, I wasn't ready to see it, because I didn't yet care to. I wasn't inquisitive about how the larger political and social realities of Oklahoma City created and sustained homelessness for particular people more than others. I wasn't that interested in the dynamics of the housing market, or the ways that people found their way into homelessness, addiction, or jail. At the time, I only had eyes to see "homeless people in need of serving."

And while that picture is incomplete, and will be interrogated shortly, it was enough for me at the time to simply recognize that people experiencing homelessness were not terrifying, nor were they exotic. They were people I went to church with, people I ate with, and people I served with, sometimes in exciting ways and sometimes in very boring ones. Though I would have to relearn this lesson again, and am often retaught it to this day, I will always be grateful for the leveled ground I walked on in that old church. In one of my first weekly reports on my internship there, I wrote something that still rings true for me today: "The only thing more profound than feeding the home-less is eating with them."

Seeing myself in the story

While Penn Avenue was changing my view of what it meant to serve people experiencing homelessness, my academic studies were teaching me to see the Bible, and thereby the whole world, in a brand-new way. My classes took me to parts of Scripture I hadn't spent much time with before, such as the Minor Prophets of the eighth and seventh centuries BCE, whose primary pro-nouncement (read: judgment) was that the people of God were neglecting the poor and the outcast. I spent time in the gospel of Luke and its specific lens on Jesus' teaching; how when Jesus said "Blessed are the poor" and "I have come to preach good news to the poor," he wasn't using *poor* as a metaphor for those with a spiritual deficit—he actually meant "the poor"! I studied the book of James, the under-preached epistle that absolutely eviscerates the rich and commands a more holistic approach to caring for the poor. The gospel, I was learning, was what Jesus said his mission was in Luke 4:18–19—"To bring good news to the poor. . . . To proclaim release to the captives and recovery of sight to the blind, to let the oppressed go free, to proclaim the year of the Lord's favor."

After I finished my degree and my time in Oklahoma City, I moved to Los Angeles to continue my theological education at Fuller Theological Seminary. There I was again steeped in a renewed understanding that God not only cares deeply about the poor, but also calls the church to entirely reorient its priori-ties to theirs; what liberation theologians call "God's preferential option for the poor." My exposure to the liberation theologies of Latin Americans (Gustavo Gutiérrez and Leonardo Boff) and Black Americans (James Cone) ignited in me the sense that serving the poor was not only a Christian thing to do, but the very essence of who God is. As Gutiérrez writes, "To be followers of Jesus requires that [Christians] walk with and be committed to the poor; when they do, they experience an encounter with the Lord who is simultaneously revealed and hidden in the faces of the poor."[1]

By the time I graduated seminary, I'd gotten married and needed to start something resembling a career. I had been changed by my reintroduction to the gospel, and this expanded my imagination for my calling. I sought out homelessness services with the expressed mission of making Los Angeles a better place for everyone, especially those who were forgotten and ignored. I had learned to see homelessness differently, to see the gospel and the world anew. However, an aspect of my vision still needed correcting: my own reflection, and where I needed to fit into the story.

I had been reading the writings and biographies of people like Dorothy Day, Bryan Stevenson, Greg Boyle, Fred Rogers, and Paul Farmer, all people with a deep connection to faith who found themselves serving outside the traditional church setting, but nonetheless doing justice work that would make the Old Testament prophets smile. One of the unintended consequences, though, of reading books by and about "heroes" and letting them inspire me was that, even unintentionally, it made me want to be more than just faithful—it made me want to be a hero too.

And as much as I can attest to the sense of calling, direction, and affirmation from God in choosing homeless services, I must also confess saviorism and a hero complex that hung over my early days of working at The Center. This complex affects many pastors, social workers, and others in helping professions, often without them realizing it. It's something I find myself having to remember to lay down even still today.

The danger of this mindset is that it is inherently othering and hierarchical. Especially for those who work with the economically vulnerable, it sets up a dichotomy of "us," the financial and moral superiors, who graciously serve "them," the people who need our help. It's a power dynamic that gets reinforced by the gratifying nature of service—we feel good about ourselves when we serve and help others, regardless of whether our impact is long-lasting or even remotely liberating. When you combine that with your peers' amazement at the work you do, it can lead to a constant reinforcement that you are right and holy in your work, regardless of the outcome.

When this dynamic is left unchecked, it becomes harmful, positioning the helpers so high above those being helped that they end up making decisions about what the recipients *actually* want or need, and eventually what they deserve. Those who already have all the power get to make decisions for the powerless. The ungodly hierarchy of rich over poor silences the unhoused and presumes to narrate their experiences for them.

Perhaps I hadn't yet read enough liberation theology to recognize that my role was not to lead but to support. Or maybe I wasn't reading closely enough about my heroes to see the through line of loneliness, self-doubt, and decentering in all their stories. (Dorothy Day's memoir is titled *The Long Loneliness*, speaking not only to her belief in the healing power of community, but also to her own doubts and isolation.)

In this way, I lovingly caution anyone approaching this work of ending homelessness, or any justice issue, to undergo serious self-examination for these biases, privileges, and complexes that can get in the way of lifting up and centering those without power. If, as Gutiérrez argues, the Lord can be encountered in the faces of the poor, then we must commit to listen to, advocate for, and ultimately join the unhoused in their own pursuit of better circumstances. This ultimately comes down to what we see ourselves as in the story: savior or servant?

When was it that we saw you?

The righteous will answer him, "Lord, when was it that we saw you hungry and gave you food, or thirsty and gave you something to drink? And when was it that we saw you a stranger and welcomed you, or naked and gave you clothing? And when was it that we saw you sick or in prison and visited you?" And the king will answer them, "Truly I tell you, just as you did it to one of the least of these who are members of my family, you did it to me." Then he will say to those at his left hand, "You that are accursed, depart from me into the eternal fire prepared for the devil and his angels; for I was hungry and you gave me no food, I was thirsty and you gave me nothing to drink, I was a stranger and you did not welcome me, naked and you did not give me clothing, sick and in prison and you did not visit me." Then they also will answer, "Lord, when was it that we saw you hungry or thirsty or a stranger or naked or sick or in prison, and did not take care of you?" Then he will answer them, "Truly I tell you, just as you did not do it to one of the least of these, you did not do it to me." (Matthew 25:37–45)

These famous lines identify the "least of these" with Jesus himself and go on to proclaim the promise of judgment resting on how we treat the hungry, naked, sick, imprisoned, and stranger. It is an awe-inducing claim, that each and every vulnerable person we encounter is Christ himself, and that how we treat them affects eternity. Every time we see an unhoused person, we are seeing Christ himself.

This claim is so audacious, in fact, it makes me wonder how much would change about our theology if we treated this passage as seriously as we treat *other* passages that talk about judgment and eternal life, including John 3:16. Between Matthew 25 and the parable of the rich man and Lazarus in Luke 16, Jesus seems far more concerned with how we treat the poor than with what or how we believe as a measurement of our faith.

But even among those of us who take Matthew 25 seriously and have a heart for justice, we may still fall short of seeing the marginalized as if they were Jesus himself. Most often, Matthew 25 is used to encourage Christians toward charity, volunteerism, and a general disposition of kindness when encountering someone experiencing homelessness. These are all good things that I think Christians should do; however, if we truly believed that each person experiencing homelessness was Christ, those things would be considered the very floor of our calling, not the ceiling.

As someone who has had to interrogate his own sense of saviorism in this work, I reflect on this passage often. It serves as a constant reminder that if each unhoused person I meet is Christ, then not only am I called to be kind and to offer help, but I am called in many ways to sit at their feet—to listen, to learn, and to change. I may still play a monumental role in helping them; my access, capacity, time, energy, and expertise may be crucial in overcoming barriers to improve the quality (and length) of their life. But I must never mistake the role I play and the skills I can offer as more than what they are, and must never leverage them for power or control in the relationship. If each unhoused person is Christ, that leaves room in the relationship only for those willing to serve, to partner, to understand. When we encounter Christ in the face of the poor, we shouldn't so much seek to transform them, but to be transformed ourselves.

This unorthodox view, which has been articulated by advocates, activists, and the unhoused themselves for decades, disrupts politics as usual. It is a rebuke to the traditional conservative notion that unhoused people just need to "pull themselves up by their own bootstraps." It forces us into relationships with the individuals experiencing it, melting away our assumptions and the myths that make it possible to believe that homelessness is a choice made by fundamentally lazy people. Likewise, it provokes the traditional liberal approach, which will spend billions of dollars on programs meant to help but that are inaccessible and misdirected because they never incorporated the perspectives, desires, and participation of the people they were designed to serve. If every unhoused person is Christ, we are beckoned into an actual relationship with people that eschews traditional power dynamics, and from which emerges two key questions: "What do you want or need?" and "How can I help?"

Additionally, if every unhoused person in our city is Christ, we are called to ask larger questions of the city itself. If Los Angeles has sixty thousand unhoused people, and each of them is Christ, we must ask questions and form strategies that address the problem on a large scale. This should never be separate from the individual, relational work of being close to the poor themselves; the choices we make on a larger scale are informed by what we learn at the feet of the poor where we meet Christ face-to-face. In later chapters, we will address more of the systemic causes of homelessness, but we can do so faithfully only if we see Christ in the faces of those who are harmed by bad policy and reprehensible cultural mores.

We should come to recognize the overall patterns and dynamics that put (and keep) people in the position of home-lessness even as we focus on the unique stories and personhood of the individuals we meet. Christ is both *each* and *every* one of them.

"Resistant"

Nicholas used heroin to manage the pain of living. One of the most vicious things about heroin, a highly addictive opioid made from morphine, is that when you stop using it, the with-drawal is excruciating. What goes up must come down, and many people, upon experiencing the pain of the drug leaving their system, seek relief by immediately using again or by switch-ing to an "upper," never really attaining a state of normalcy. But Nicholas's supply was out, and he was wallowing outside The Center's front gate, unshaded on a hot summer day. He had been out there over an hour, refusing to talk or move, before he finally spoke. "I need help. I want to go to treatment. I can't do this anymore."

You would think these words would have been music to my ears, but I was wary. Maybe it was because it was three in the afternoon on a Friday—social workers like weekends too—or maybe it was because I knew where this was probably headed.

Choosing to stay optimistic, I went inside and spoke with our clinical director. He made some phone calls, pulled a few strings, and got Nicholas a bed at a detox center. He even offered to drive him down there.

"Down where?" Nicholas asked, skeptically, when I relayed this news.

"It's in Skid Row," I said, reluctantly.

His answer was gruff and instantaneous. "Never mind."

Nicholas got up and walked his bike away. I couldn't blame him.

Going to rehab in Skid Row is like going to a dentist in the middle of a candy store. You might do everything you went there to do, but the moment you walk out you're right in the middle of your worst nightmare.

We can't blame the dentist for setting up in the candy shop, though. After all, that's where the most need is. Most of the resources in Los Angeles go to Skid Row because it has the city's largest density of people experiencing homelessness.

In the wake of the devastating impact of the 2008 recession, Skid Row couldn't expand much further, because of ongoing gentrification in downtown, so homelessness exploded across LA. Many people simply started their experience of homelessness in the neighborhood where they had rented or owned. However, all the needed resources to serve them, such as rehabs, detox centers, and housing, continued to mostly be welcomed only in Skid Row. Through a combination of denial, contempt, and misunderstanding, neighborhoods across LA refused time and again to establish necessary resources in their own communities.

A byproduct of this community-wide stubbornness is that people like Nicholas often get labeled as "service resistant." This moniker saddles so many people experiencing homelessness, most often used by service providers and politicians to draw distinctions between groups of people experiencing homelessness: those they believe they can help and those they consider unhelpable. But in the story I just told, who was truly "service resistant"? I would argue that neighborhoods, not Nicholas, deserve that label.

Nicholas's story is not unique—the myth of service resistance distorts the way we see homelessness as a culture. I once listened to police officers describe a whole encampment as service resistant because they had pulled up in a squad car and offered everyone there shelter beds and were told no—never mind that the shelter they were offering was seventeen miles away in an entirely different community. Unhoused people depend on patterns of knowing where to get food, clothing, showers, and other resources within walking distance, and they were being offered an overnight bed somewhere they had never been. This claim of service resistance also ignores the poor reputations of many shelters, and the lack of trust that the unhoused community has with those offering it—the police. Would you accept an undesired offer from the same people who wrote you multiple tickets in the past week for living on the sidewalk?

When this "service resistant" label gets applied to a large portion of the population, it is used to justify actions we may not normally accept as humane. It is a resignation, often a duplicitous one, to give neighborhoods and cities the justification they need to make unhoused people disappear—moving them to another block, another neighborhood, another city, or just to jail. Because of our failure to truly see homelessness, we drive people experiencing it out of sight.

In all my years of working in homeless services, having met thousands of individuals experiencing homelessness, I have never once met a truly service-resistant person. I have met people who did not want to talk to me, who cursed me out, who told me to go to hell and any number of other things when I have offered them particular services at particular times. But never once have I formed a relationship with someone whose true, authentic desire was to live on the streets and subsist on charity and handouts. When I've met those knee-jerk responses that many take as a final answer, I always try to dig deeper: What are they truly saying no to?

Perhaps, like Nicholas or the encampment approached by police, they're saying no to the location or the environment of the services. Maybe they are saying no to the rules that come with the program being offered; many shelters have curfew policies that any adult would feel patronized by. Maybe they are saying no to you, the asker, because they don't trust you. I've seen programs let people down time and time again. I've seen golden housing opportunities taken away over technicalities or last-minute funding changes. I've seen promises broken, lies told. Behind every person's no is a history about which we likely know very little.

A colleague of mine is known to say, "People are not service resistant; services are people resistant." In this reversing of the aphorism, we are invited into a new way of seeing what really goes on when someone refuses services. We are always quick to question and denigrate the person, but we rarely ask questions about the services themselves, or the person offering. What does it say about the services we are offering that people would rather live on the streets than accept them? Civil leaders and service providers should see a flurry of no responses as saying more about them than about the unhoused population.

It isn't just political leaders and nonprofits who think and talk this way, though. I've heard it from people whose family members are homeless: "We've offered/tried to help and they don't want it." Having spoken to many people who are disconnected from their families, it is much more likely that they don't want *their* help, not that they would refuse any help whatsoever. I've also spoken with people who have developed a relationship with a specific unhoused person, who sleeps near their work on their church property, with similar conclusions. But without knowing a person's whole story, the specific services being offered, and the world of trauma and experience behind the no, we cannot see people as "service resistant." (And this is to say nothing of the role that mental illness can play in distrust of services, which we will look at more in chapter 5.)

In most cases, if unhoused people were actually offered desirable services in a preferable area, with no barriers and no strings attached, by someone with whom they've built rapport and trust, even the most "service resistant" would take the offer happily. This is actually a proven approach that we will examine more in the next chapter. When we see unhoused people as people with stories, preferences, and desires, labels like these become inadequate, even inhumane. We should not use these easy and dishonest categories to excuse ourselves from our commitment to ending homelessness, especially as people who follow Christ.

Seeing and sinning

God cares deeply about who we see, and how we see them. As we've explored, this theme emerges throughout Scripture, but perhaps never as explicitly as in John 9, the story of Jesus healing a blind beggar.

"As [Jesus] walked along, he saw a man blind from birth" (v. 1). Jesus *saw* a man who *could not see*. Right out of the gate, we are clued in to how "seeing" will be a central theme of this story: who can see, who can't, and the implications therein. After Jesus sees the blind man, his disciples ask Jesus the key question for the rest of this chapter: "Rabbi, who sinned, this man or his parents, that he was born blind?" (v. 2). This passage is about seeing, but it is also about sinning.

While there isn't an exact analogy between Jesus' time and today for persons experiencing homelessness, as so many contextual factors differ, this story might get us the closest. Being blind, this man was unable to earn a living. If he was begging, we might be able to assume that he was disconnected from his family—perhaps by death. As it stood, he was in a position where his physical disability left him unable to provide his own means for survival, and this left him on the margins of the community begging for its pity and charity.

Despite these differing contexts, this question—"Who sinned?"—is no less culturally ingrained in us now than it was in Jesus' time. So often our perception of homelessness is skewed by a bias toward the assumption that poverty (and homelessness by extension) is the result of a moral failing. This isn't uniquely Christian, but as we saw in the introduction, it is more rampant within our churches than outside them. Like the disciples, we see homelessness and ask, "Who sinned, that this person ended up this way?"

The instinct is a defensive one. We see a person experiencing unimaginable suffering, and we try to make sense of it by finding someone to blame. The easiest and most comfortable answer is to blame the person. If they bear the blame, we no longer bear the responsibility of helping them. If they are guilty, they become unworthy of our assistance. We use sin and shame to free ourselves from the responsibility of bearing one another's burdens.

The truth about homelessness is that there are a lot of ways to end up there. Asking how people become homeless is like asking how people end up in the hospital. There are a lot of avenues, some of which are irresponsibility, negligence, violence, accidents, bad luck . . . but we would rightly be shocked to hear a doctor say, "It's your own fault, so you're on your own!" It might be useful for a doctor to ask how you ended up with your injury or illness—it may in fact help the doctor treat you—but it should not be a determining factor for whether you are treated or how much treatment you receive. Whoever ends up in the hospital deserves to get well, as does everyone who experiences homelessness.

Jesus' response to this question is stunning. He says, "Neither." And then he heals the man. To Jesus, a person's future is not dictated by what they have or have not done in the past. Jesus practices grace, interrupting and disregarding all our petty logic about who deserves what.

It is crucial that we understand this point if we are to understand grace as it applies to homelessness. The belief that people deserve homelessness because of bad choices they've made is pernicious inside and outside the church. Many of the chapters to come in this book will argue that the claim "People experience homelessness because of character defects rather than external factors" is completely misguided and untrue. But even if it were true, if we take grace seriously, *it doesn't matter*. Like Jesus in this story, we are called as Christians to be uninterested in someone's past as a determinant of their future. A quote commonly attributed to Dorothy Day says it best: "The gospel takes away our right forever to discriminate between the deserving and the undeserving poor." Jesus is disinterested in deservedness. He is singularly focused on healing.

The story isn't over, though. There's still a punch line coming regarding this connection between "seeing" and "sinning." When the man tries to tell the Pharisees the good news, they reject him and send him off, declaring him "born in sin" and without the right to teach them anything. After hearing of this rejection, Jesus insists, "I came into this world for judgment so that those who do not see may see, and those who do see may become blind" (v. 39).

The Pharisees retort, "Surely we are not blind, are we?" And Jesus delivers the punchline: "If you were blind, you would not have sin. But now that you say, 'We see,' *your* sin remains" (v. 41, emphasis added).

The chapter began with the disciples looking at a blind beggar languishing on the streets and asking "Who sinned?" The passage ends with Jesus telling only the Pharisees, "Your sin remains." In Jesus' worldview, those in need are the ones who get to see, and the self-righteous religious folks are the ones unwilling to see the world through God's eyes.

When we cast judgment—on the poor, on the persecuted, on the marginalized, when we intentionally elevate ourselves morally over someone else, claiming that they are getting what they deserve—it is we who are subject to the judgment of God. What ails *them* is far easier to treat than what ails *us*. When we see pain and ask "Who sinned?" the answer is *us*.

New glasses

Here's a sentence I never thought I would write in a book about homelessness:

Spoiler alert for the Marvel Cinematic Universe.

And yet working among those experiencing homelessness is full of surprises, and one day I found myself texting this to Michael, whom I had helped house: "So in *Ant Man and the Wasp*, Ant Man goes to the 'quantum realm' which is a place you can shrink so small that space and time no longer exist. At the end of that movie he gets stuck there. Enjoy *Endgame*!"

Fans of accurate science may not appreciate that text, but fans of superhero movies might. One of the things I learned about Michael during the process of navigating him into housing and then working hard to keep him there was that he *loved*

Marvel movies. Which was wonderful, because so do I. Unlike me, though, Michael was not caught up, so to speak. At the time there were twenty-three movies in the Marvel Cinematic Universe, of which Michael had seen several but not all. He was eager to know what happened in the epic films for which he'd seen numerous billboards and trailers, especially *Avengers: Infinity War* and *Avengers: Endgame*—the two-part box-office smash that was the culmination of over a decade of inter-connected movies.

On a Saturday in January 2020, I was taking Michael to pick up some brand-new bifocals. He had never worn glasses in his life, but his vision had begun to deteriorate over the past year. We had previously taken him to a free, government-funded dental and eye care event, where it was determined that Michael needed bifocals, and his eyes were tested to identify the exact specifications that would enable him to see clearly.

It took ten long weeks for the bifocals to be ready, and we had to drive from Hollywood to Compton—almost twenty-five miles—to pick them up, another all-too-familiar story of services not actually matching the needs and circumstances of the people they're for. Had I not had email access to find out where and when the glasses were finally available, and a car to take Michael across the county, and the flexible schedule to do so on a Saturday (when very few case managers work), Michael would have waited all that time for nothing.

The frustration of it all went away the moment he put them on. I hadn't seen him that happy since the day he got keys to his apartment. On the way back, he read aloud random road signs and advertisements just because he could. About halfway home, I revealed my surprise: I had secured copies of *Infinity War* and *Endgame* on DVD to watch when he got home. We stopped for lunch, and he ate like a man with a singular purpose: to get home as soon as possible.

I made him promise to text me in between the two movies because he needed a few details from a movie he hadn't seen that came out in between. *Infinity War* is two hours and twenty-nine minutes long, and I am not exaggerating when I say that Michael texted me no more than two and a half hours after I dropped him off. He had wasted no time. So I sent the above text, and laughed to myself about how delightfully absurd my job is sometimes.

The most fulfilling moments of my work happen when the power dynamics of worker and client, or of privileged and needy, melt and give way to true human connection; when, with coffee mugs in hand, we bond over a favorite song, laugh together at a bad joke, or geek out over superhero movies. In so doing, we lay a foundation of safety and trust on which we might build something special somewhere down the road. When we relinquish the part of ourselves that wants to play the hero, and instead bring our whole, true selves to the work, the way is paved for us all to experience transformation together.

In these moments we see and are seen by one another, connected through the small but indispensable pieces that make up our unique and whole selves. These connections have transformed how I see homelessness and those experiencing it, rinsing from my eyes the false belief that unhoused people deserve their circumstances, or that they are helpless without me. Grace, like a new pair of glasses, allows us to see every aspect of homelessness differently.

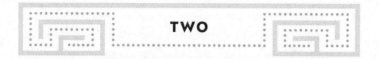

TWO

Housing

ONE ORDINARY TUESDAY, I met Javier. He had come to our gate midafternoon, well after our programs had ended for the day. As is often the case for those coming to The Center for the first time, he knew little about us and what we could offer, but he'd heard we could help.

For the first time in his life, at ninety-one years old, Javier was a week away from homelessness.

I would come to learn that he had worked steadily in good jobs from his late teens into his seventies. He had retired with a pension that allowed him to live comfortably. He had lived in the same place for the past twenty-five years: a small one-bedroom apartment, as he had never married. At ninety-one, he had outlived all the family he had ever known. About five years before I met him, his building had been purchased by a development company. Each year they had been raising the rent by a couple of hundred dollars. Each year he found ways to make his fixed income go further to continue covering this rent: cutting unnecessary costs, relying on food banks, and using utilities as little as possible. Despite his resourcefulness, eventually the math just wouldn't work anymore, and he paid what he could until the eviction notice came.

Housing is a consistent theme in Scripture, and the language of "home" and "dwelling place" permeates our songs and liturgies. Yet the actual realities of housing are so often ignored by churches, which prefer to consider this language spiritually rather than literally. We cannot afford to do this, though, because housing is inextricable from the topic of homelessness. Having learned to see those who experience homelessness as neighbors worthy of care, respect, and dignity, the temptation is to stay focused on addressing homelessness one person at a time. Even Christians who lead with compassion and dignity in their daily interactions with unhoused people are often reluctant to make the leap and see homelessness as a systemic issue with systemic solutions. For this reason, before moving to individual encounters and local aid programs in the next chapter, I am intentionally drawing our attention to homelessness on a macro level. This is because I believe that Christians are called not simply to "manage" homelessness, but to end it.

If we want to talk seriously about homelessness, we first have to talk about housing. The only thing that every person experiencing homelessness has in common is that they do not have access to sustainable housing. This sounds obvious, right? It's right there in the words: home*less*ness, *un*housed. And yet housing is a touchy subject for many. More than simply where we live, housing in the United States and Canada is an industry designed to generate profit. For a few, housing is a profiteering enterprise; for many who own the home they live in, it is a source of financial and emotional stability. In both cases, whether they are defending astronomical profit-making or simply their own sense of security, there is a vested interest in moving the conversation away from housing.

Yet neither the data nor the gospel allows us to ignore the way that housing inequity and injustice creates and perpetuates homelessness. The good news is that there are proven, replicable, and scalable models to end homelessness with housing. We do not have to reinvent the wheel, but can simply join alongside a movement already in motion. This movement is entirely congruent with the values of our faith as given to us in Scripture, especially through the life and witness of Jesus.

It will require us to interrogate our biases around what people deserve, and to consider the cost of being wrong. If we are to make a lasting impact on homelessness, we need to establish a Christian ethic of housing that aligns with the best practices learned through decades of organizing and trial and error, and that reflects the character and desires of the Creator of the land we have claimed, divided, and developed.

Homelessness

Lack of affordable housing causes homelessness. The connection is definitive, provable, and irrefutable.[1] The jury is not out on this matter. States with higher rent costs have more homelessness. Los Angeles always ranks near the top, though locals like to say that unhoused people flock to cities like Los Angeles for more preferable outdoor weather. This has been largely disproven—the vast majority of people experience homelessness in the same neighborhood or city where they were most recently housed.[2] And the speculation also fails to account for the significant rates of homelessness in cities such as New York City or Seattle.

This doesn't mean that everyone in the same location is equally at risk for homelessness. As housing and homelessness researchers and policy experts Marybeth Shinn and Jill Khadduri put it, homelessness is the result of a "cascade of events and a cornucopia of risk factors."[3]

Homelessness is the intersection of housing affordability and poverty, and poverty can result from a variety of interweaving realities. While my rent in Los Angeles is more than double my sister's mortgage payment in Arizona, I am at little risk of homelessness thanks to my resources, community, and connections. My safety net is strong—mostly for reasons that I did not work for or choose.

It's important to acknowledge that many of the things we associate with homelessness, such as disability, mental illness, or substance use, do not themselves *cause* homelessness, but rather are risk factors that increase vulnerability to homelessness. Additionally, we associate them with homelessness because they are realities that worsen without housing—a decrease in mental health and an increase in substance use are extremely predictable results of a person being without stable housing. In more affordable areas, these same risk factors exist but don't represent an automatic plunge into homelessness. The state of Mississippi, for example, boasts the lowest cost of living in the United States and its lowest rate of homelessness. When people in Mississippi experience the same risk factors, rent remains relatively affordable, homelessness is avoided, and this stability affords people the means to alleviate other concerns.

All these elements reflect choices that we make. The decision to allow factors like disability, mental illness, and substance use to result in homelessness is centered on policies, not individual failures. It is a policy choice to allow rent costs to soar while wages remain stagnant. It is a policy choice to allow disability benefits to be dwarfed by the cost of a studio apartment. It is a policy choice to allow buildings where seniors live on fixed incomes to be purchased by developers who raise the rent beyond what the tenants can afford. It doesn't have to be this way.

Merit-based models of ending homelessness

For almost a century, we've been using a model to address homelessness that does not work. The old model goes by several different names: treatment first, housing readiness, or the staircase model. I will refer to it as the merit-based model, because it ultimately asks unhoused folks to earn their way toward help. Under this model, a person must demonstrate compliance with a particular treatment plan, rules, and supervision to graduate to the next step toward permanent housing. From the streets, individuals often have to be clean and sober or medicine-compliant to stay in a congregate shelter.[4] In the shelter, they have to obey rules like curfew to keep their spot. From the shelter, they can enter a program that can graduate them to interim housing, often with roommates. These programs require ongoing treatment, attendance, and sometimes, religious requirements such as attending a Bible study. Only once these terms have been successively met can one hope to graduate to independent housing. Each step must be earned, and those who finish the program in its entirety are celebrated and held as exemplary, while those who do not are often deemed "not ready" or, as we've already explored, "resistant."

Several problems arise with this methodology. Unfortunately, faith-based organizations continue to be some of the strongest proponents of this model. This merit-based system operates under a belief that the primary issue facing the unhoused is not material, but spiritual. In 1996, the executive director of the International Union of Gospel Missions wrote of emerging government programs, "They refuse to challenge the homeless person's fundamental way of thinking. . . . Most significantly, these programs ignore the central dimension of the problem—the spiritual."[5] While it is important and necessary to take a whole-person approach to homelessness, this belief really ends in only one place: blaming individuals for their own homelessness.

As we saw in the previous chapter, this belief leads to so many damaging outcomes for the unhoused, including criminalization. In a recent podcast with *Christianity Today*, the current CEO of Citygate Network (formerly known as the Association of Gospel Rescue Missions), which empowers and supports more than three hundred Gospel Rescue Missions across the United States, called on churches to stop feeding people in the park, and explicitly supported the criminalization of homelessness as an incentive to drive people to transformation:

If we're going to solve this, we have to change a lot of these lax laws that are allowing people to remain homeless and be comfortable. . . . What's missing here is a sense of responsibility. Because of our desire to be humane, we have taken away any sense of responsibility from people who are on the street. Yes, there's mental illness and there are addictions that have to be treated, but if you don't have a sense of responsibility and you don't feel some sort of pain from living this lifestyle, then we're going to see more and more people there.[6]

Additionally, Gospel Rescue Missions hold evangelism as a key goal, believing that accepting Christ is crucial to overcoming the spiritual flaws that lead to homelessness. And because Gospel Rescue Missions hold such a historically dominant place in the landscape of shelters in America, this fusion of the merit-based approach to housing with evangelism has made it not only the dominant Christian approach, but also our wider cultural response to the issue. It leads us to believe that people experiencing homelessness deserve to be miserable, alone, and in pain until they are willing to accept our conditional, coercive help. In the name of conversion, we have developed a model that is the opposite of God's freely given and freely accepted grace.

More than being morally and theologically deficient, this approach also simply does not work. Its proponents use a self-fulfilling prophecy when celebrating its successes: *If only everyone had the discipline and fortitude to finish the program, it would work for everyone.* From a statistical standpoint, this model cannot meaningfully address homelessness. Having studied this approach and its outcomes, Shinn and Khadduri reach a damning conclusion: "The data seem to show that the treatment-first programs did not change people so much as they sorted them into those permitted to come indoors and those relegated to the streets."[7] In fact, the percentage of people accessing these shelters who go on to graduate and attain housing is lower than the percentage of people who resolve their own homelessness without any assistance. The vast majority do neither.

Calling "transformation" what is more accurately conformity or assimilation, these programs denigrate the worth of the vast majority of unhoused people to uphold their flawed belief system. Because this approach has dominated the landscape of services in both religious and secular programs for decades, few people have been able to succeed, and millions more have been unfairly labeled resistant to help of any kind. And since, during these same decades, rent costs have increased while wages and safety nets have remained stagnant, it has relegated the individuals with the highest needs and barriers to the streets.

This can account for the confusing reality that while most people believe homelessness has been growing worse, the number of people experiencing homelessness in the United States has been rather consistent for decades. Homelessness is not worsening in quantity nearly as much as it is worsening in quality of life. While services cherry-pick the easiest or most willing to cooperate, those who remain worsen in health, mental health, and substance use, making their road to wellness longer, and certifying their status among the general public as "undeserving."

In the past thirty years, however, we have found a better way. This new approach continues to be proven effective at ending homelessness on a large scale, demonstrates success in housing and stabilizing people who were deemed unhelpable, with dignity and mutuality, and actually saves money in the long run. We call this the Housing First model.

Housing first

New York Times bestselling author and host of popular podcast *Revisionist History* Malcolm Gladwell wrote an influential article on homelessness in 2006 called "Million Dollar Murray: Why Problems like Homelessness May Be Easier to Solve Than to Manage."[8] In this piece, Gladwell highlights a particular unhoused man named Murray in Reno, Nevada, a man known for his kind heart, toothless smile, and unrelenting, costly addiction to alcohol.

In the piece, Gladwell examines the issue from a cost-benefit perspective. The moniker "Million Dollar Murray" refers to the cumulative cost of Murray's constant arrests, hospitalizations, treatments, and other adjacent expenses, costs which were ultimately incurred by the city. "It cost us one million dollars *not* to do something about Murray," observed a police officer who frequently interacted with him. In Murray's case, it would have been cheaper to give Murray a house and a nurse than to keep cycling him through jails, hospitals, and sobering centers.

Gladwell argues that committing to housing the people whose homelessness is most severe will wind up saving money in the long run. In addition to the emergency response, we spend billions each year on managing homelessness by funding nonprofits, policing encampments, cleaning streets of debris and human waste, and so much more. The article ultimately poses a question that advocates have been asking with increased frequency and volume: If we are already spending billions to manage homelessness, why not spend the money to end it?

Having known and cared for dozens of Murrays over the years, the cost-benefit analysis is far, far down the list of reasons I support changing how we approach homelessness. The point is essential to understand, though, because it provides an answer to the foremost rebuttal to policy changes: "But how much is it going to cost?" The great news is, it doesn't cost any more than we already spend! This enables us to ask an even better question: "What values and outcomes will dictate how we spend our money on homelessness?"

When it comes to these values and outcomes, nothing beats the Housing First model.

Pioneered by Dr. Sam Tsemberis, the founder of Pathways to Housing, this approach has revolutionized homelessness services globally. After localized success within its own program, Housing First has been evaluated by multiple studies. It continually demonstrates success in helping the most vulnerable individuals attain housing and keep it.[9]

Drawing on many of the values that we've already established, this approach abandons the old merit-based model and moves people directly from the streets into permanent housing. It is built on the following principles:[10]

1. *Consumer choice*: The individual experiencing homelessness has options as to the type and location of the housing. Additionally, services like mental health support, addiction treatment, and medical services are constantly offered but always voluntary.

2. *Community-based*: Housing and services are rooted in the local community, not sent "somewhere else."

3. *Mobile support services*: Services are nimble and can be brought to the participants when possible, rather than requiring them to seek them out.

4. *Permanent housing*: Participants have their name on a lease, and are able to keep their housing for as long as they want it—housing is "a human right, not a privilege to be earned."[11]

5. *Harm reduction*: Rather than mandating transformation for problematic behaviors or realities, the focus is on minimizing and mitigating the harm that results from these behaviors. (We will discuss this approach extensively in upcoming chapters.)

These values align with the demands of grace: that love is freely given and noncoercive; that people are met where they are, not where we wish they would be. I don't know whether the pioneers of this model have roots or attachments to faith, but I see the love of God permeating it all the same. This is one of the fundamental reasons I believe this model works.

Finland has all but eradicated homelessness using this model. It's beginning to catch on and spread to other parts of Europe with early signs of success. Smaller cities and communities throughout the United States have applied Housing First to a particular subset of their unhoused population—such as veterans, youth, or chronically unhoused—and have ended homelessness for that group.[12] On a larger scale, the city of Houston cut its unhoused population in half in under ten years, and brought veteran homelessness to functional zero, a term used to describe when homelessness is so manageable that any instances that do arise are brief, rare, and nonrecurring.[13] Housing First works, and it is scalable.

Bypassing the usual steps of the merit-based model, and not requiring participants to prove their worth, Housing First immediately works to find housing that matches the wants and needs of people experiencing homelessness. The only expectation is that people pay 30 percent of their income for rent, a percentage that has for a long time been understood as the maximum amount any individual or family should spend on housing in order to afford all other necessities. If their income is zero? Until a case manager can help secure income, their rent is zero. Once housing is secured, that person is offered personalized resources and services, which are entirely voluntary.

This is often the sticking point for detractors: Why should services be voluntary? If we're giving people so much for free, can't we expect *something* in return? But to this thinking I ask, Don't we want people to get better, even if we have to force their hand a bit? I will suggest a few reasons why this contentious point is crucial.

First, forced treatment almost never sticks. Regardless of whether someone is forced into rehab, detox, or mental health treatment, relapse rates are incredibly high. In a study comparing Housing First to Treatment First, where the former did not require sobriety and the latter did, there was no difference in the outcome of who still used substances and who didn't. Requiring sobriety did not produce sobriety in the program's participants; it produced only "dropouts"—that is, people sent back to the streets for failing to comply.

When individuals themselves are not willing, free participants in their care, it is almost impossible for meaningful change to take place. Just because we give housing first doesn't mean we default to the methods of the merit-based model, leveraging housing to produce the change we want to see in a person. Treatment has to be chosen without coercion or threat in order to be truly effective.

We find ourselves once again confronting an assumption we have seen emerge several times already, that people experiencing homelessness do not want help. We are so accustomed to believing that unhoused people do not want to do anything about their mental health or addiction that we think services must be mandated or else people won't take them. Time and again, though, I have seen people desperate for these services who simply don't have reasonable access to them, or who do not have the stability to complete them.

This leads to the second and perhaps most important point: For people experiencing homelessness, housing itself is the most meaningful intervention for virtually all other ailments. Unsurprisingly, for someone with a chronic health condition or disability, housing provides stability that soothes many symptoms of the physical ailment. Wheelchair users or people with breathing conditions or chronic pain will all experience better physical health outcomes if they are able to go to sleep each night and awake each morning in an apartment rather than on the streets. If you've ever had to do physical rehab after an injury or surgery, imagine that process without a home to return to each day—rehabilitation requires stability.

The same applies to those with mental health and substance use disorders. Stable housing provides respite for symptoms ranging from minor depression and anxiety to psychosis. When people attain housing, their substance use decreases. As we will explore further in the chapters about mental health and substance use, homelessness escalates the harm of these barriers, and housing reduces them. While it does not eliminate those barriers, housing also provides a baseline of stability for a person to be able to access and participate fully in helpful services.

Continuously offering services that are accessible, local, and personalized remains an essential piece of Housing First. We assume the best of people—that they want to improve their lives and well-being—while also recognizing that housing itself *is* treatment, and that enthusiastic participation in healing is the only path to true transformation.

In this way, housing ends homelessness. Housing provides stability whereby people with other barriers and vulnerabilities can work on them more effectively. With services provided, those barriers and vulnerabilities can be managed, minimized, or eradicated in ways that are all but unimaginable from the streets. When people feel safe, they can truly flourish.

Following a theology of grace, we believe that we are loved *into* healing, not loved *because* we are healed.

Theology of land and housing

Housing First works, and it can functionally end homelessness. If we are to implement it successfully, though, we have to address a few housing-related issues that significantly influence the success of Housing First programs.

Ultimately, ending homelessness means entirely reevaluating our theological relationship to housing, property, and land. As Christians, we often take for granted the significance of "place," but the story of the people of God has always been deeply concerned with where we live and how we live there.

In *The Land: Place as Gift, Promise, and Challenge in Biblical Faith*, biblical scholar Walter Brueggemann presents the history of land and landlessness through Scripture as a key prism through which to understand God and faith. In our tendencies to spiritualize and existentialize faith, we forget that so much of the story of God and God's people is rooted in land, land that is promised, exiled, and reclaimed. How the people of God relate to land is a fundamental aspect of biblical theology.

In examining this motif, Brueggemann concludes that land is understood as either "gift" or "grasp"—we either grasp at land to possess it and use it to our advantage, or recognize it as gift and manage it "as an arena for justice and freedom."[14] The warning of Scripture is that those who grasp at land will lose it, and those who understand it as a gift will find it. Those who understand that the earth is the Lord's, and not theirs to possess solely for their own use and benefit, are those who recognize that the meek and the poor will inherit the earth: "Biblical faith," writes Brueggemann, "is the reminder to us that those [dispossessed] voices may well be the voice of God himself allied always with the dispossessed against the landed."[15]

As we align ourselves with best practices for ending homelessness for those experiencing it, we need to examine how our relationship to land and housing works toward or against that goal.

Homelessness prevention and eviction

In 2018, Los Angeles housed more people than it ever had before. The homelessness services delivery system, of which The Center is a part, housed more than twenty-one thousand people in a single year. In that same year, however, an estimated fifty-four thousand people became unhoused. Despite herculean efforts, primarily guided by Housing First practices, more than twice as many people fell into homelessness than were able to be supported out of it.[16]

If Housing First is to work, we need to address the economic conditions that are generating homelessness at an unmanageable rate. The boat is filling with water faster than we can scoop it out. Rising housing costs are a huge part of this, and we will shortly turn to a discussion of affordable housing. But first we need to examine one of our most entrenched and catastrophic housing-related practices: evictions.

After doing a thorough, personal study of housing instability in Milwaukee, sociologist Matthew Desmond wrote *Evicted: Poverty and Profit in the American City*, a seminal work on the exploitative practices of eviction and its disastrous consequences. Desmond highlights how eviction as a practice has spun wildly out of control, amounting to millions of evictions each year. In these proceedings, 90 percent of landlords are represented by lawyers, whereas 90 percent of tenants are not.[17]

The ability to evict with impunity often puts tenants in a precarious power dynamic, leading to underreporting of poor living conditions or exploitative practices.

Eddie Glaude tells a harrowing story of eviction in his book *Democracy in Black*: Police swarmed a foreclosed home in Atlanta at three in the morning to evict sixty-five-year-old Christine and her family, carelessly scattering all their belongings on the front lawn and forcing them to pack, she said, "as if I just had a fire." That night, most of the family slept in their car. As Christine recounted, "When they came for me at three in the morning, they didn't have a place for me and my family to go, but the animal shelter came because they knew that there were dogs there. They came with a place for my dog."[18]

In a country that's become increasingly comfortable with housing as a profit-driven enterprise rather than a basic need or human right, evictions have run rampant. They have become a default practice rather than a last resort, inflicting pain and violence on people who are already at their most vulnerable. With one in five Americans and Canadians paying more than 50 percent of their income on housing, more of us are closer to the brink of homelessness than at any time in the past century.[19] While moratoriums have largely delayed an overwhelming flood of evictions anticipated because of the economic fallout of COVID-19, this dam will most certainly break without a comprehensive intervention.

If we are to reduce the flow into homelessness, we need to rethink our stubborn overreliance on evictions. We need to support people who are on the cusp of eviction to be able to remain housed, or help them relocate to a more sustainable situation. This can be a primary point of entry for Christians and churches: interrupting the cycle of homelessness before it begins.

Housing First is great at ending homelessness, but it can do little to prevent it. For far too long we have allowed housing to be snatched away from the most vulnerable and willfully ignored the aftermath—seeing unhoused people as lazy, immoral, or otherwise undeserving rather than as victims of a detestable system and practice. Matthew Desmond, the son of a preacher, concludes his analysis of the ramifications of the eviction crisis by exhorting, "No moral code or ethical principle, no piece of scripture or holy teaching, can be summoned to defend what we have allowed our country to become."[20]

Affordable housing and NIMBYism

It should go without saying, but Housing First as a methodology works only if there is enough housing to offer. The shortage of affordable housing drives many into homelessness while also creating an environment where the best aspects of Housing First cannot be put into practice. I've seen this firsthand in Los Angeles—while local officials celebrate Housing First principles, too many people are competing for the few available units. To determine who should get them, we institute rules, qualifications, and barriers that undermine the principles.

The National Low Income Housing Coalition reports that "only 37 affordable and available rental homes exist for every 100 extremely low-income renter households" across the United States.[21] The figures are even lower in high-density cities like Los Angeles, New York City, and Washington, DC. To prevent homelessness in the first place, and to apply the best practices for ending it, we need enough affordable units to match the demand.

It's hard to explain the current homelessness crisis without focusing on key policies of the 1980s. The Reagan administration

gutted most funding for public housing and aid programs, causing an astronomical loss in the country's supply of low-income
housing that was never replaced. Additionally, the administration removed or minimized social safety nets for the most
marginalized. The net result was an increase in people at risk of
homelessness, and fewer affordable units to house them. Many
sociologists and historians mark this period as the beginning of
homelessness as we know it today[22]

One of the biggest obstacles to new affordable housing is
NIMBYism. NIMBY is an acronym for "not in my backyard,"
a rendering of the common sentiment that while many people
want the poor to be housed and to have services, they don't
want it to happen *near them*. Even where funding and advocacy
for affordable housing is high, NIMBYism prevents it from
coming to fruition, citing concerns for safety and decreasing
property value as the primary objections. This appeal to safety,
often centering around proximity to children, is a powerful
rhetorical tool that does not match reality. It echoes the arguments once used for racial segregation, ultimately being more
about our prejudice and discomfort than about any actual evi-
dence of a change in the neighborhood's safety. NIMBYs may
in fact be right to fear a decrease in property value, though this
is still often overstated. The value of a property may not increase
as exponentially as it otherwise might if it is in proximity to
affordable housing, but it likely will not plummet. Still, allowing affordable housing in your neighborhood comes with a cost.

For Christians who are homeowners, property managers,
even landlords, our calculus must be different. Rather than
leveraging these privileges to bless ourselves through wealth,
we are invited to see them as opportunities to participate in
God's mission to liberate the oppressed. And yet NIMBYism

runs deep within Christian traditions that equate property and land ownership with blessing and merit. However, a biblical theology of land affirms that regardless of claims of ownership, "the earth is the LORD's and all that is in it" (Psalm 24:1; see also 1 Corinthians 10:26). Nowhere in Scripture are we promised wealth-generating property. Whatever land or property we find ourselves in control of, we are called to steward it with our Christian values first and foremost. In this way, Christians should always reject NIMBYism, for it was never our backyard to begin with.

Churches, denominations, and faith-based educational institutions, too, have a responsibility to prioritize an ethic of land stewardship. These larger Christian entities are responsible for an enormous percentage of land and property in the United States and Canada. Putting this land to use toward ending homelessness may be the single greatest contribution that communities of faith can make.

Many are already answering this call. My home church has used its space to provide temporary housing for evicted families, and many members have taken in individuals in the midst of housing crises. Churches I know have purchased vacant properties to convert to housing. Others have donated unused land, or sold buildings to the city at reasonable prices to develop low-income or supportive housing. Still others allow nonprofits to use their sanctuaries during the week, or their parking lots to be used for "safe parking" (a supervised overnight parking space for people living in their vehicles).

Despite this range of opportunities, far too much land, space, and housing goes underutilized. Churches who steward large properties should seriously consider how their property can be creatively used to address housing crises in their neighborhoods. If property is sold, attention should be paid to who is purchasing it and what their purposes with it will be; a development company seeking to build luxury apartments may make you an offer you "can't refuse," but perhaps living into God's mission means taking less money for the good of the city and its unhoused residents.

Housing is the key to ending homelessness. We have to drastically expand affordable housing and universally adopt Housing First to ensure it is maximized toward ending and preventing homelessness. We must reject "solutions" to homelessness that require people to earn or demonstrate their worthiness for our help, even those advocated by faith-based organizations, not simply because they are inconsistent with a Christian ethic, but because they do not work. Research reinforces that a compassionate, Christlike approach to homelessness *is* the most effective at resolving the crisis we're in. We can move in confidence in our conviction that every unhoused person is worthy of help and care, and can advocate for solutions that respect the image of God in all of us and deliver solutions that alleviate suffering.

THREE

Isolation and Connection

A LOCAL PASTOR recently asked my advice on how to help a particular woman experiencing homelessness. She had been a member of the congregation and surrounding community for years, and the church had actually helped her get into a housing program. Unfortunately, as is too often the case, the program didn't match her needs, and she had recently returned to the streets after about a year of being tenuously housed.

"It just kills us to see her sleeping at the park again. But I don't know what else we can do," the pastor said with a sigh.

Even among those of us who believe in and fight for housing justice, there remains a question of what we do about homelessness *right now, today*. Policy change, building and repurposing housing . . . these things take time. Meanwhile, there are people on the streets this very moment with a variety of needs too urgent to wait for these larger structural changes to take place.

What I told this pastor—and this is something I believe wholeheartedly—is that genuine solidarity, communion, and friendship is possible with people who are currently experiencing homelessness, even as we fight to end it. Homelessness is not a black hole, swallowing people and putting them out of our reach. Rather, unhoused people are ready for, and in need of, connection and friendship. They are our neighbors; the very same that Jesus calls us to love in the same way we love God and ourselves.

This chapter and the next aim to respond to the questions that likely drew you to this book: How do I interact with and respond to people experiencing homelessness in the here and now? For many of us who live in larger cities, this question emerges daily as we find ourselves face-to-face with unhoused people seeking assistance. Others who participate in charities or ministries that serve people experiencing homelessness may wonder whether there isn't a next step or a better way. Others still may be looking for their entry point into the work, something more grounded and actionable than the big-picture ideas of the previous chapters.

Solidarity and friendship with unhoused people is essential, and these relationships can interrupt some of the most harrowing aspects of life on the streets for individuals. This examination extends into the next chapter, where I emphasize responses focused on creating and sustaining community with and among the unhoused. Both of these chapters identify isolation as a key problem and connection as its solution. My tendency is not to dictate *what* to do, but to suggest *how* to go about doing it.

While I do hope that some Christians and churches will respond to new and exciting models for solidarity and kinship with the unhoused, we will continue to need people of faith to provide basic needs like food, clothing, and shelter. For those who wish to start or continue these more traditional kinds of work, there is still an invitation to incorporate models and practices of connection and community to make your work even more humanizing and to promote the flourishing of the most vulnerable.

Isolation

In the Genesis narrative of creation, God calls everything that God makes "good." In the whole story, there is only one thing that God describes as "not good"—that anyone should be alone. We have long recognized that loneliness has spiritual ramifications, on top of so many others.

In a recent study, 92 percent of unhoused youth in LA identified "fragile social networks" as the cause of their homelessness.[1] This is of key importance: Falling into homelessness requires more than just financial or resource loss. If I lost my job and my bank account were dry, my network of family and friends would prevent me from having to spend the night outside. With such an overwhelming number of people on the streets, we recognize that not everyone has access to that same support.

We can identify another key cause and contributor of homelessness: isolation. With unaffordable housing and the presence of other risk factors playing their obvious roles, isolation is a consistent thread in the stories I hear from people. Themes of loss, betrayal, exclusion, distrust, and abuse always emerge when people share how they ended up living on the streets. Homelessness is not simply a loss of housing, but also a loss of connection.

Isolation is not only a *cause* of homelessness, but also an aggravator. Once people begin sleeping outside, they become instantly disconnected in official ways (like no longer being able to receive mail) and implicit ones (like being disregarded by people who avoid speaking to them or even looking their way). This isolation makes the experience of living outside all the more demoralizing, and dangerous.

When isolation becomes prolonged, it can have catastrophic health ramifications. In isolation, physical health and mental health deteriorate. People are less likely to go to the doctor when they are sick or unwell, or even to be aware of the severity of their health issues.[2] As these conditions worsen, people are less and less likely to want help and support, and less able to seek it out if they do. With exacerbated physical and mental health complications, substance use can become a means for self-soothing and pain management. Isolation becomes a very quick, slippery slope into crisis, resulting in catastrophe. Even in California, where the weather is considered more livable, the life expectancy for an unhoused person is forty-seven years, nearly half the state average of eighty-two years. Homelessness is, in effect, a death sentence.

This should create in us an urgency not only to address homelessness on a grand scale with housing and long-term services, but also to triage and intervene for those who are most isolated, at risk, and languishing on the streets. At the heart of these interventions is the need for authentic human connection. While unhoused people can and do form genuine connections with one another,[3] individuals, churches, and service providers must build the trust and safety that allows for timely introduction of life-saving services and treatments—the types of things a stable social network would typically provide.

Most of our interactions with unhoused people are defined less by intentional connection than by incidental contact— we are often caught on our back foot in encounters we didn't anticipate, unequipped to respond in the way that may be needed. Most often our interactions with unhoused people are in public when we're running errands, or in service settings that don't lend themselves to genuine connection. But with some intentionality, these dynamics can be transformed.

What do I do?

Among people who know what I do for a living, I get asked one question more than any other. Whether I'm with extended family at Thanksgiving or talking to a stranger at the gym, they want to know one thing: what to do when a person experiencing homelessness asks them for money.

This question has probably been on your mind too. You may even be wondering why I waited until the third chapter to address it. This is intentional. For one, a holistic view of homelessness and how to end it should inform how we engage with individuals experiencing it—we can't treat homelessness case by case without understanding the larger dynamics at work. Moreover, it's important as Christians to recognize that our call is to engage and dismantle systemic injustices *because* they are unjust, not because they inconvenience us or cause us to have uncomfortable interactions.

Let me assure you, though, that it is okay to feel awkward in these encounters. It can be helpful to remember that the person asking is also likely uncomfortable—imagine being in a similarly desperate position, facing both the likelihood of failure and the necessity of success. In these interactions, it can feel as if so much is at stake. We are confronted with a moral choice that seems to carry the whole weight of a systemic problem; as though how we respond—or don't respond—is representative of our whole ethos around homelessness.

Even after five years working in direct service, I still get anxious when asked for money. I still feel guilty when I say no—I don't want to come across as cruel or uncaring. I want to shout and signal to everyone, "I actually care! I *really* don't have cash, I swear!"

As unavoidable as the shame and guilt is, we need to give everyone grace in these situations, including ourselves. The key advice I give to everyone who asks boils down to three things: boundaries, assumptions, and acknowledging humanity.

Boundaries

As a culture, I don't think we talk enough about boundaries. In homeless services, though, we talk about boundaries *all the time.* Because the demand for resources so greatly exceeds the "supply," boundaries are absolutely necessary. There is not enough housing, case management, food, or clothing to go around, and certainly not enough time to provide them at the rate at which people need them.

I remind all our new hires of a sobering truth: If you and I and everyone at our organization worked twenty-four seven for the next year, we would not solve homelessness in Los Angeles. In fact, we would actually burn ourselves out after a week, tops, and we'd be of no use to anyone. Boundaries means saying no to some things so that you can say yes to what's most important.

Boundaries need to be in place *before* we need them. Even though these situations happen over and over again, we wind up entering each one just as unprepared and flustered as the last time. Instead, as individuals or families, we should thoughtfully predetermine our boundaries around homelessness so that we can enter any encounter with confidence. A great place to start is to ask, *How am I responding to the crisis of homelessness in my neighborhood or city?* This may include giving in some situations when people ask, or it may not. But establishing an answer to this question can help alleviate some of the pressure inherent in these interactions.

If you do decide that there are certain situations where you may give money to people who ask, it's important to clearly know which situations dictate a yes and which ones don't. For myself, I will never say yes if I am in Hollywood, because that's where I work. Someone might recognize me as working at The Center, or see me there later, and now I've potentially created a relational dynamic that is harmful for our organization and what we're trying to do. However, I don't live in Hollywood, so when I am out in other neighborhoods, my boundaries are different. Typically, if I have cash, I will give it to someone if they ask.

For my own moral clarity, I try to make this a blanket policy so that I don't allow any unconscious biases to affect the question of whom I give to and whom I don't. These biases can be gendered, racial, or even as seemingly innocuous as how "clean" someone is or my assessment of their mental health.

Everyone needs to develop their own boundaries—identifying which ones are rigid and which are flexible. Maybe you are like me and want to specify certain areas where you will or won't give. Maybe you will make it dependent on whether you have cash, whether you are alone, whether you are in a hurry; maybe you'd rather give food, a gift card, or some other resource like socks or a hygiene kit. Boundaries may be based on a number of different factors and concerns, and we should always make sure they reflect compassion and honesty.

Assumptions

Without a doubt, many of our boundaries are based on assumptions about homelessness and the people experiencing it. As we develop our personal boundaries, we must do so in a way that is thoughtful, with an eye toward the truth. It's often helpful to reflect after an unsettling interaction has happened. A good question to ask is, What assumptions guided my responses?

A common refrain I hear among those who do choose to give goes something like this: "It doesn't matter what they do with it, that's between them and God. But whether or not I give, that's between *me* and God." I agree with this approach to an extent; it shifts us away from obsessing over whether a person deserves the money that you give them and cultivates a posture of generosity. At the same time, it puts a whole lot of existential weight into interactions that, for those of us who live in big cities, happen too frequently to consider so clear-cut.

On the opposite end of the spectrum is the widely accepted assumption that people asking for money are putting it to nefarious use, specifically to purchase drugs or alcohol. We don't have data on this, but anecdotally I can suggest that this concern is not well founded. For one, the notion that your money might be the difference between someone using drugs or getting clean is quite silly. Despite knowing hundreds of people struggling with addiction, I've not once heard someone say, "I was about to give up and stop using heroin forever, but then that nice lady gave me ten dollars and I was able to score." That is simply not how addictions work. Only larger interventions like treatment, healthcare, and housing can interrupt something of that magnitude.

It is also the case that a gift of money is extremely unlikely to end someone's homelessness. Except in very rare circumstances, panhandling is not a way to get out of homelessness, but rather a way to make it less miserable. Your money may not purchase an apartment, but it may buy someone a clean pair of socks. It may afford them the dignity of a meal at their favorite restaurant after a day spent hungry. It may buy a weekend in a hotel to get off the street and out of the elements. These are not nothing! Your gift may not lift someone out of their desperate situation, but it might provide an incredible amount of solace and even joy in the midst of despair.

Above all else, homelessness dehumanizes. It isolates, it discards, and it amplifies fear and anxiety. In your daily interactions with people experiencing homelessness, their homelessness is not truly at stake. Their humanity, though, is.

Acknowledging Humanity

Whether you interact with an individual experiencing homelessness or don't, a lot is communicated regardless. I hear from unhoused people all the time how keenly aware they are that people look away, change course, and avoid eye contact. These are impulses that we act on both consciously and unconsciously. I'm convinced that we do these things because homelessness itself—more than the individuals experiencing it—scares us. We are afraid to reckon with the way our economy and society churns out victims, and it's easier to just not look.

But if we could look, what a difference it would make. If we went against our impulses and made eye contact, perhaps even smiled or nodded at one another, acknowledging our shared existence and humanity, we all might just become a little more human in the process.

For those who don't wish to give, but do want to be kind, I recommend a very simple phrase: "I'm sorry, I can't today." This communicates remorse, and that you recognize their need but are unable or unwilling to meet it. You make it clear that you are not going to give, and without having to overexplain or justify it. You also leave open the possibility that you may give another time. (If it's not within your boundaries to give, you can leave off "today.") Nearly every time I use this phrase, it is received and understood graciously. If the person responds with a salutation, I return one, and a human interaction has taken place with no harm done. While no situation is entirely predictable or without anxiety, I have found these steps help me make good decisions that are sustainable, are built on truths about homelessness, and respect everyone involved.

Trauma-informed care

For the first few months Mark came to The Center, before I had even started working there, he never said a word. Staff would ask him his name as he entered, but he would simply walk past them to the coffee urn. After a few months of hanging around in silence, he shared his first name. A while later, his last. By the time I started working there, he would say hello and goodbye; he would come to discussion groups we held, but would just declare "Pass!" when it was his turn to speak.

Fast-forward five years, and the man will hardly stop talking. In groups he goes off on long, fantastical tangents that at times have to be reined in so others have a chance to share. He asks thoughtful questions. He recounts in near perfect detail the plots of movies he watched at the library but wildly misremembers the movies' titles. (Some memorable ones: *Paddington* became "Pinkerton," *Jumanji* was "Jubongi," and *The Magnificent Seven* became "The Seven Magnificent Guys.")

In the same way that Mark was initially slow to open up to us, he remained slow to accept help and resources. Despite keeping a meticulous routine to access every possible meal within walking distance (which for him could be up to fifteen miles), Mark generally did not want to talk about his needs. Nonetheless, we always offered him opportunities when they came along.

It was no minor shock to us the day he agreed to see a Medi-Cal enrollment specialist. We had just opened a satellite medical clinic on-site and were setting people up with primary care. He sat with the specialist for almost an hour, and for the first time in as long as we'd known him, Mark was connected to a primary care physician—ours. He began meticulously attending weekly appointments, even agreeing to take medication to mitigate some health concerns. He has become the foremost advocate for his own care, showing up early to appointments, and handwriting notes for me to pass along to his physician as reminders to refill his prescriptions.

What a change from the guy who never said a word. We'll continue to offer him endless opportunities and see what he will be willing to trust us with next.

Mark's story is an extreme example, but one that highlights the essential aspects of providing opportunities for people to move out of isolation and into connection: low barriers, patience, consistency, and mutual trust. More often than not, people warm to this posture more quickly and begin to lead the way toward their own wellness. If we begin from a place of radical acceptance and partnership, there is no obstacle too great to overcome.

The methodology at work here is called trauma-informed care, and while it has become ubiquitous in social work and many educational settings, it has yet to make many inroads into church practice. And this is a shame—trauma-informed care not only meets and recognizes people amid their brokenness and pain as Christ modeled, but also emphasizes a spirit of collaboration and empowerment. As we examined in chapter 1, our role in the story is not to be a savior but a servant.

The most important aspect of this methodology regards the first word in it: trauma. Trauma is the result of "exposure to an incident or series of events that are emotionally disturbing or life-threatening with lasting adverse effects on the individual's functioning and mental, physical, social, emotional, and/or spiritual well-being."[4] When we recognize the role that trauma plays in shaping people and their behavior and responses to help, it fundamentally changes the way we see and treat unhoused people. In short, it enables us to love better. One training on trauma-informed care I attended described this as "unconditional positive regard"—not unlike the way we understand how God loves.

When we see people through the lens of unconditional positive regard and recognize the role trauma plays in each of our lives, we are able to interpret behaviors and responses differently. When someone we serve has an outburst of anger, violates a boundary, or seems uncooperative, trauma-informed care reminds us that these are responses and coping mechanisms that a person resorts to in order to feel safe and okay. Instead of dismissing people as resistant, difficult, or hostile, it allows us to understand *why* a person is behaving a particular way. It shifts the conversation from "That guy is just a jerk" or "She is just lazy and doesn't want to be helped" to more empathetic, more accurate thoughts and questions:

> He must be having a bad day.
> Something about this situation may be setting him off.
> I wonder what barriers are in her way to accepting help.
> What would it take to build trust with her?

The final key to trauma-informed care is safety, which holds radical acceptance in tension with boundaries and limitations. Trauma stems from occasions of violence or danger—whether physical, sexual, emotional, or otherwise—when the person's safety was not guaranteed, and is triggered by moments that remind the person of that same feeling. Some of these triggers are so unique and specific to a person's experience that we can't always anticipate what might be a trigger; but the key to developing trust and making progress with people is ensuring that they feel as safe as possible.

Safety is more than just providing a space that is absent of physical danger. It also means not pushing people socially, emotionally, or spiritually. Returning to Mark as an example, many programs may not have allowed Mark to enter without giving his name. Others may have eventually discontinued serving him because he didn't participate at a dictated pace. Still others may not have bothered to offer him resources, because they knew he wouldn't go as far as they needed to demonstrate successful outcomes. Thankfully, The Center's use of the trauma-informed care model enabled Mark to move at a speed that felt safe.

Our service delivery systems are still often far too quick to rule people out for demonstrating textbook responses to trauma. While we strive to keep everyone safe above all else, it remains imperative when serving the most vulnerable that we do not use negative behavior as a reason to cut people off from much-needed services. This doesn't mean that any and all behavior is tolerated or that there are no consequences. Instead, it means that safety, rather than punishment, is the driving factor in response to negative behaviors. With this approach, I have eventually been able to serve and help people who have attempted to choke me, who have thrown chairs at coworkers, and who have cursed at and threatened me. In all these cases, violations were addressed in restorative ways that acknowledged the harm done and put new boundaries in place, but that allowed each person to eventually regain access to services. This is how we, a secular nonprofit, practice the transformative forgiveness that Jesus returns to again and again in his teachings.

Social psychologist Henry Stack Sullivan famously said, "We are all much more simply human than otherwise."[5] Bringing humanity in all its pain and beauty to the forefront allows us to see people as God sees them, and to thus respond with empathy and care to the complex realities that people present to us. These trauma-informed responses move us away from judgment, labeling, and exclusion toward radical acceptance. Within that acceptance, even the most isolated and traumatized can move toward connection and flourishing.

Flourishing and friendship

> *So you say you love the poor? Name them.*
> —Commonly attributed to **FR. GUSTAVO GUTIÉRREZ**

After decades as a psychotherapist, Dr. Irvin Yalom believes that successful therapy ultimately boils down to the relationship between the therapist and the patient, regardless of the mode of therapy used. He concludes, "It's the relationship that heals."[6] Yalom also suggests that this healing works in both directions, that both the client and the therapist experience restoration through the therapeutic relationship.

Some of my favorite work moments would have been impossible if not for this reciprocal understanding of relationships with the unhoused people I meet. To laugh and joke, reflect and mourn, see and be seen is possible only where space has been intentionally carved to get to know one another as humans on a journey together, not as those who serve and those who are served.

During a particularly busy drop-in time, a longtime participant named Phinoy rounded a corner and yelled to me, "Kevin! Someone's looking for you!"

"Who?" I asked, a little flustered.

"Your barber." A wry smile crept over his face. I bowled over with laughter. Never before, and never since, have I been so unexpectedly, strategically, and lovingly roasted.

Another time, a young hopeful-musician named Jimmy told me I looked like Mr. Incredible. I took it as a compliment, until a few months later, after I'd lost some weight while training for a race, he added, "Remember how in *The Incredibles* at first he can't fit into the suit? You fit your suit now, Kev!" I wore an Incredibles shirt to work that Halloween to keep the joke running.

This relationship-first approach takes intentionality. We are accustomed to providing goods and services to people, and are often met with gratitude and the feeling that we've done good. And we have! But knowing the deadly effects of isolation on unhoused people who are subjected to it, I believe that for every ministry and program designed to serve the unhoused, there is also an opportunity, and a responsibility, to prioritize relationships.

Are there places for people to stop and rest for a bit while receiving services, or do people have to grab and go? When providing food for people, do they have an opportunity to sit and eat comfortably and slowly? Do they get to engage with staff and volunteers beyond the transaction? For as much as homelessness services are built on transactions, moving away from a transactional model and emphasizing a relational one goes a long way. This isn't a call to stop giving tangible resources or serving food, but simply to reorient the way in which we do so to prioritize relationships and connection.

At The Center we have a steady stream of volunteers, and when they arrive they often ask what they're supposed to do. They're looking for a task, a station, or a role. Most often, I redirect their desire to *do* and encourage them to simply *be*. I send them to our patio, where dozens of unhoused people have gathered to drink coffee and socialize, with the singular purpose of having conversations. When I debrief with these volunteers afterward, they are amazed at how quickly their nervousness gave way to comfort, and how much their perception of homelessness changed by simply talking with people who experience it as human beings.

For Christians and churches looking to do something with and for the unhoused in their community, creating spaces that draw people in for fellowship and connection can be one way of meeting a need that many service providers are unable or unwilling to do. As you begin this work, take the time to learn what tangible resources already exist in the area, and build on what's still needed rather than duplicating or reinventing them. For those who already have active ministries, consider how you use space, time, and people for building relationships rather than transactions. Look for ways this is already happening and see how you can strengthen it. Identify aspects that may be preventing or undermining authentic connection, and address them.

In pursuing relationship and connection, we emulate the ministry of Jesus. In the midst of providing miracles of nourishment and healing, Jesus frequently shared long meals and conversations with all types of people. He did this so often that he was criticized by both his opponents and his friends for being "a glutton and a drunkard" (Luke 7:34). Jesus was committed to slow, relational work—knowing that connection is a healing force that moves us all toward wellness, flourishing, and transformation. The church, at its best, offers the basic human needs of connection and relationship in a world that is increasingly isolated and numbing.

Churches are resourced theologically and tangibly to support connection and relationships, inviting people experiencing homelessness out of isolation in ways that are life-giving, and even life-saving. For as long as people remain unsheltered and vulnerable to the dangers of homelessness, the church can prioritize the safety and flourishing of people while we work toward permanent solutions.

FOUR

Community and Solidarity

LATE ONE NIGHT in the spring of 2021, over four hundred members of the Los Angeles Police Department descended on Echo Park Lake, one of LA's most iconic outdoor landmarks, to erect a fence. After months of contention with the park's unhoused residents and housing activists, the city council-member with jurisdiction over the park had decided to clear the park under the guise of "renovations." Once the fence was up, those who had been living in the park were given twenty-four hours to leave under threat of arrest.

The encampment at Echo Park Lake was more than just a random cluster of tents. It was a thriving community, built on mutual aid, solidarity, and care. The residents had constructed a community kitchen and a system for receiving and distributing resources equally, and had even rigged working showers. The residents were well connected with advocates and activists who lived in the surrounding neighborhood, which allowed for quick response to emergencies and crises. It reminded me of the early church described in Acts, who "were together and had all things in common" (Acts 2:44).

The encampment had even reached out to local officials to ask for things they needed. While the surrounding neighborhood was complaining about the park's cleanliness, citing an over-flow of trash and human waste, the encampment was actively advocating for access to bathrooms and a dumpster. They were met with silence or outright antagonism—an employee came at sundown every night to lock the park's existing bathrooms. The group was also clear that the park was not their last stop but merely an exercise in making the most of a bad situation, as they remained focused on housing as the ultimate goal.

The forceful displacement of the encampment at Echo Park Lake raised for me fundamental questions about community, solidarity, and connection with unhoused communities. How do people experiencing homelessness engage in and with com-munity? How do we honor our unhoused neighbors' commu-nities while still offering a way out of homelessness and into housing? And where, in all this, can the church lean in to its own communal structure and traditions to embrace unhoused communities in solidarity?

Encampments

There's no mistaking that encampments make housed people nervous. We may not want to admit it out loud, but this is a truth I have observed time and again. A single tent next to a neighborhood or business may be thought of fondly; people know the inhabitants by name and interact with them regu-larly. But when one tent becomes two, three, and on up from there, the mood turns. Fondness turns to fear, connection to avoidance, and compassion to resentment. Perhaps one person feels manageable in a way that multiple do not. Or maybe it's because multiple people produce more trash and noise.

Whatever it may be, it's important that we acknowledge it. Then we need to change it.

Encampments are crucial to the well-being and survival of people experiencing homelessness. They provide safety, support, and community for the most vulnerable in ways our system does not. Encampment residents save each other's lives by quickly responding to overdoses and other health crises. People in encampments organize shifts to supervise belongings so people can attend appointments and work toward getting off the streets. Food, clothing, and cell phone chargers become shared resources. I've witnessed encampments offer refuge to women fleeing abuse. One of the former residents of Echo Park told me, "Just 'cause we're on the street doesn't mean we have to be miserable. We can have a decent life, a good quality of life . . . just because we have each other."

For case managers, encampments provide a consistent location to connect with their clients. The process of moving off the streets and into housing is long and arduous, but when good news comes it's important to act fast. When people live in consistent encampments, not only do we know where to start looking, but we know a whole group of people who are likely to know where they are.

I do not mean to cast encampments as uniformly supportive utopias. As with any given community—churches included—a variety of structural and interpersonal dynamics can combine to make an encampment either healthy and vibrant or toxic and dangerous. However, the ability for unhoused people to develop communities and networks of support within and among themselves should be recognized and supported rather than scorned. More to the point, if our primary reaction to these communities is antagonism, whether structural or personal, their ability to become healthy and vibrant is stunted.

Sadly, we let our fear and resentment of encampments lead us to pursue criminalization and displacement. Through a variety of anti-homeless laws, cities and states and provinces and neighborhoods prevent people experiencing homelessness from being able to establish a consistent home base. When we choose to displace people, belongings such as medicine, identification, and paperwork required for housing get lost in the shuffle and discarded. When communities are scattered, people become isolated and distrusting of services, losing faith that anyone is interested in actually helping.

All housing is sacred

One of my earliest revelations working in homelessness is a phrase I've kept close to my heart: Housing is spiritual. This little idea cuts through the false dichotomy that is so often demonstrated when Christians look at my "secular" work and ask, "But what are you doing for your participants' *spiritual* needs?" Housing is more than a roof, a door, and walls; it is spiritual, it is sacred.

Writer Hannah Bowman explicitly applies this to the makeshift dwellings of encampments: "Whether you're using bricks or canvas, on your own property or on a sidewalk, the making of a home is a sacred act."[1] She connects the temporary encampments of unhoused people to the makeshift dwellings of the people of Israel while in exodus and exile, and how that way of life was honored and is still remembered. For example, the Jewish festival of Sukkot, also known as the Feast of Tabernacles, remembers when the people of Israel lived in makeshift dwellings in the wilderness after the exodus from Egypt. One of the traditions of remembrance is to build a sukkah, a makeshift dwelling like those used, and spend a night in it.[2]

Believing that all kinds of housing are sacred and spiritual isn't the same as saying they are equal. It means that we approach different types of housing with a sense of humility and curiosity—learning what people value and cherish about their situation and what they would like to see change or improve. We are quick to identify what we think is missing from encampment living, ignoring the sacred lives and communities that people build despite their situation. Once again, we are so quick to set ourselves up as the experts on the experience of homelessness rather than seeking the direction of the true experts: those who live it. If we take time to listen and see the good that's already there, we can reach solutions that are dignifying and desirable.

This approach was modeled with great success in El Sereno, a neighborhood northeast of Downtown LA. Huntington Drive, a primary artery of Los Angeles's interconnected roads and highways, runs through El Sereno with two lanes in either direction, with an unusually large, grassy median known as "the Island." Over time, the Island had become home to close to one hundred unhoused people, culminating in a community response.

This story did not end as it did in Echo Park, with fences and SWAT teams. Instead, Union Station, a nonprofit in the area, was granted two local hotels by the city to serve as permanent housing for the Island's residents.[3] Outreach teams built trusting relationships and helped move residents into the hotels without ultimatums or coercion. By partnering with the people they were working with, they had a nearly 100 percent success rate in convincing people to move in. Building on the community's existing sanctity and maintaining clear paths of communication, Union Station was able to permanently house hundreds without incident. In a display of solidarity, the new residents voted alongside staff to rename the buildings Casa Luna and Huntington Villas.

This kind of story should be the norm, not the exception. If we can look at encampments and see not a scourge but sacred communities of people trying their best to survive, surely we can find creative solutions to build on the resilience and solidarity already present among people experiencing homelessness. In so doing we affirm that all housing, however temporary, is spiritual.

Marginalized communities

In talking about isolation, connection, and communities, we must address how particular demographics have been systematically excluded from access to resources, both tangible and intangible, that relate directly to housing stability. The demographics of homelessness, when compared to the general population, demonstrate that homelessness does not affect all people equally. This is largely the case because the primary predictor of homelessness—access to affordable housing—has been shaped so profoundly by prejudice.

The ways people are discriminated against on the basis of race, gender, sexual orientation, and gender identity have a direct impact on the landscape of homelessness. Marginalized groups within these categories experience homelessness differently, both qualitatively and quantitatively. Homelessness does, in fact, discriminate—because we do.

We cannot adequately address homelessness unless we reckon with these patterns of excluding marginalized people. This section will by no means provide an exhaustive understanding of how homelessness interacts with members of these groups, or easy answers for undoing centuries-long patterns of discrimination. I offer it instead as a means for deeper understanding, reflection, and a call to action. The church should be leading the way when it comes to enacting restorative justice for marginalized peoples—even (and especially) where the church has been explicitly responsible for their marginalization.

Discrimination based on race

This section focuses on Black Americans, who statistically bear the overwhelming burden of systemic racism in the United States,[4] and highlights myriad ways that race intersects with homelessness for all people of color, and how systemic racism affects their risk for, and experience of, homelessness.

In their analysis on homelessness in America, the Center for Social Innovation reported what many of us have seen with our own eyes: Black people are vastly overrepresented among the unhoused. All things being equal, we should expect that any demographic's representation in the general population would be reflected in the unhoused population. Instead, while representing just 13 percent of the general US population, Black Americans account for 40 percent of the country's homeless population. White people, on the other hand, account for 74 percent of the general population but only 49 percent of those experiencing homelessness.[5]

Knowing that homelessness is primarily an issue of housing access, it becomes obvious that our history of housing discrimination is a direct cause for this disparity. In the past century alone, explicit and implicit practices of housing discrimination have left Black Americans more vulnerable than any other people group to housing insecurity. White soldiers returning home from the Second World War were greeted with easy access to no-money-down, low-interest loans to purchase or renovate homes, while Black soldiers' access to the same loans was severely restricted. The practice of redlining, too, highlighted a national strategy of racial segregation by denying loans and preventing investment that would go toward renovations and community development in non-white neighborhoods. The neighborhood in which I now live was commended in 1940 by the California Real Estate Association as "being worthy of singular praise in its utilization of measures to keep it a '100 percent Caucasian Race Community.'"[6]

While the Fair Housing Act of 1968 outlawed outright racial discrimination in housing, data show that discrimination still occurs to this day. A peer-reviewed study on rental discrimination in 2003 showed that a Black applicant with no criminal background is less likely to get a callback on an application than a white applicant with one.[7] In December 2021, the Austins, a Black couple, had their San Francisco home appraised at just under $1 million. Believing this to be an undervaluation, they removed all family photos from the home and asked their white friend to pose as the owner. The new appraisal came in just under $1.5 million.[8]

For the past century, as each generation of Black Americans has been systematically denied equal access to homeownership, millions of white Americans have enjoyed generous government subsidies to secure property and its accompanying advantages. Housing subsidies have been a historic benefit for those who have been deemed worth investing in—through federally backed low-interest loans, property tax deductions, and several other tax incentives.

The ongoing practice of housing discrimination means that Black people are more likely to be renters, more likely to be "rent burdened" (paying more than 30 percent of their income on rent), and therefore at greater risk of homelessness. Because housing discrimination has affected multiple generations, many Black people on the brink of homelessness are unable to count on support from their community. I've been on the phone as people reconnect with family members who desperately wish they could take in their child or sibling, but who can't afford to because they themselves rely on subsidies such as Section 8, which carry strict rules against additional occupants, regardless of family status.

Understanding how this came to be is the first step in addressing it. Rooting out racism in its many forms in ourselves, in our churches and programs, and in our laws is the next step. We can mourn the realities for how they exist, but we must do more than that—we must take up the cause of intentionally reversing these trends.

The irony here is that so often we reject the idea of subsidizing housing for the poor because of a belief that people shouldn't receive handouts. Yet in 2018 (the most recent year for which this data are available), the federal government lost out on over $148 billion to homeowner deductions and benefits while spending less than $50 billion for rental assistance, public housing, and housing assistance grants altogether.[9] Among white Americans, 71 percent own their home, compared to only 42 percent of Black Americans.[10]

Discrimination based on gender

An article published by the *Los Angeles Times* in 2016 highlighted a sharp increase in the number of women experiencing homelessness. According to this most recent count, women now make up close to one-third of the unhoused population.[11]

At The Center, this article prompted an urgent meeting among our staff; not because this new data showed an over-representation in homelessness—now it actually more closely matched the general population—but because we were alarmed that the data weren't reflected in whom we saw attending our programs. We didn't track demographics at the time, but we estimated our attendance to be more than 90 percent male. After confirming that the numbers for our neighborhood were the same as the greater LA area, we were forced to face a startling fact: hundreds of unhoused women lived in our vicinity but had remained largely invisible to us.

We began asking the women who were coming to reflect with us on why this might be, and what we learned changed the way we understood the female experience of homelessness. They told us that women frequently avoid accessing resources because of the constant threat of violence from men. On the streets, without even the basic protection afforded by walls and a locking door, unhoused women are largely vulnerable to potential attackers. Because of this, many women try to be invisible on purpose. Additionally, to avoid these types of harm, many unhoused women find it strategic to enter into exploitative relationships or social arrangements. Abuse from a partner who provides even meager shelter, food, or protection may seem the lesser of two evils when compared to the relative danger of going it alone.

To create a safer environment for women to access The Center's resources and community, we began setting aside Fridays for an exclusive "Women's Day." It has been successful in welcoming many women who were previously wary of attending. We have yet to see our ratio of attendance match the neighborhood's demographics, but our commitment to providing specific programming to meet the unique safety needs of women has become a pillar of our program's identity.

Women experience homelessness differently than men, and because of the overwhelming presence of men they avoid many services that are aimed at serving all people. By paying attention to our neighborhood, recognizing areas and people we've missed, and listening to the people we seek to help, we have been able to address that gap. Anyone involved in work that aims to help women experiencing homelessness needs to consider whether their environment creates safe, secure space for these women to access services.

Discrimination based on sexual orientation and gender identity

Christians hold a wide range of beliefs and practices when it comes to LGBTQ+ identities. In some churches, LGBTQ+ Christians are welcomed and celebrated, and in others are rebuked or in hiding. Many Christians see this as the primary battlefront of the culture war, while others see no barrier to faith for people of any sexuality or gender identity. I don't presume to know where you, the reader, fall on this spectrum, but neither can I make the costly mistake of letting any of us off the hook for everything the gospel requires when it comes to marginalized communities.

I remember talking to Eric shortly after he got his housing voucher. He knew I had gone to seminary, and he loved to talk theology and church with me. He asked me what I thought about the church and gay people. I laughed a bit as I replied, "I got in a bit of trouble with my denomination when they asked me that exact question!"

He looked me straight in the eyes with a wry smile. "Oh yeah?" he said. "Try growing up in the church and *being* gay." I listened as Eric described having a deep and abiding faith in Jesus but growing up fearful that his community would alienate him because of his sexuality. When he finally came out, his fears were realized. He decided to move to Los Angeles, away from the community that rejected him. Shortly after, he ended up on the streets with a heavy backpack containing essential items and his most prized possession: a framed photo of his parents.

This story is all too familiar. Especially among unhoused transitional-aged youth (ages sixteen to twenty-five), LBGTQ+ identities are vastly overrepresented. Like Eric, when LGBTQ+ people come out to their communities, they are driven away—when teenagers do it, it often means being kicked out of their homes. Despite rhetoric to the contrary, unhoused people statistically stay close to the communities where they were once housed. LGBTQ+ youth, however, are the lone exception, tending to leave for somewhere new, someplace that feels safer and more accepting. Metropolitan areas make for appealing landing spots because of their generally progressive cultural climates. For its part, Los Angeles may be hospitable to LGBTQ+ folks, but it is no place to be poor, and homelessness awaits many of these wanderers.

Even when these youth end up in shelters, safety remains a primary concern—including and especially for trans women. At faith-based shelters such as rescue missions, which are often explicitly non-affirming, transgender people are classified and assigned to sleeping areas by sex assigned at birth rather than stated identity. While these institutions are separated by gender for safety—in under-supervised, communal settings, women experience violence from men far more than when these groups are separated—data also show that trans women are far more likely to be victims of violence than to perpetrate it.[12] Despite talking points that have become disappointingly prevalent, trans women are not statistically likely to abuse cisgender women in these settings. However, forcing trans women to sleep in the designated men's section does put them at direct risk for targeted violence. Non-affirming theology may discriminate between a cisgender woman and a trans woman, but data show that victimizers do not.

If the intention is to keep all residents safe, the best way to do this is to allow people to sleep in areas that match their gender identity. The trans person you are serving is not attempting to sleep in one place over another to make a statement or to victimize others—they are making a calculated choice to maximize their physical safety.

As Christian institutions continue to agonize over their theologies of gender and sexuality, we cannot lose sight of the physical and psychological harm we are inflicting on people whom God loves. Our limited theological imaginations, which prioritize how we *think* and *feel* about sexuality and gender identity over how we value the actual lives of fellow bearers of the divine image, are driving LGBTQ+ people to homelessness and all its subsequent harms.

Fostering community

At The Center, our motto is "Community Ends Homelessness." We practice solidarity with the unhoused in Hollywood by providing a safe space where community can flourish and following it up with constant opportunities to engage services. We find that this value is so often missing in the world of service provision, despite how fundamental it is to the human experience, and how easy it can be to implement.

One of the ways we practice this value is by facilitating groups that create space for connection and shared experience. Over the years, we have hosted groups on mindfulness, recovery, art, writing, travel, movies, games, nutrition, music, gardening, exercise, and so much more. While life skills or self-betterment might be incorporated, these groups are not necessarily aimed at *teaching* anything, but rather seek to foster community. By partaking in the groups, people naturally build relationships with one another and with staff and volunteers, ultimately instilling hope and companionship amid the hard reality of homelessness.

When I led groups, my favorite was always Short Stories. On Tuesday mornings at ten, about ten to fifteen of us would read aloud a short story I had preselected, then take a few minutes to ponder and sip tea before entering into a lengthy discussion about the story, its characters, and themes.

What I discovered by leading this group is that stories can be a back door to our psyches. We were able to discuss heavy topics, some participants intersecting the stories with their own life experiences and traumas, and others connected with characters and stories vastly different from their own. The story and its characters functioned like an avatar, allowing us to bring our own selves into the narrative and connect with one another there at a safe distance.

It's no wonder this has actually become a therapeutic modality, known as bibliotherapy, and is used in a variety of settings, including hospitals, schools, and prisons.[13] Studies have shown that reading activates the same parts of our brain as when we are trying to understand someone's feelings. Reading is an exercise in empathy. Author Jeanette Winterson has said, "Fiction and poetry are doses, medicines. What they heal is the rupture reality makes on the imagination."[14]

Activities like reading are what give our lives vibrancy and joy, yet we are reluctant to extend opportunities like these to unhoused people, prioritizing tangible needs even though we have the capacity to do both. Because of this, it remains a challenge to demonstrate the value of our groups to the larger system of homelessness services, and especially funders. Many want to see quick, tangible results: Is this person off the streets? Did they get a job? Are they out of the system now? And yet we know that we, as humans, are so much more than this—and that so much of who we are is formed in communities.

The poor are always with you

One of the biblical passages most often deployed against the work of alleviating poverty comes from a comment of Jesus, commonly rendered as "The poor you will always have with you" from the NIV translation. The conclusion for many is that Jesus is making a claim about the future. Those who use it in this way suggest that, per Jesus' own words, there will always be poverty, and thus the work of ending it is futile.

This conclusion simply cannot be a legitimate reading of the text. The three gospels that record the story all use the verb meaning "have" in the present tense, not the future—and this is reflected in every other major translation besides the NIV, including the KJV, NASB, and NRSV. The more accurate translation that each of these other translations affirm is "The poor you always have with you." Rendering it in the future tense allows for the unhelpful reading that Jesus is making a future prediction.

Instead, as we see, Jesus is making an observation about the present. Jesus' disciples *are* always among the poor; that was Jesus' primary audience and following, in fulfillment of his mission statement, "To bring good news to the poor" (Luke 4:18). In Mark's gospel, we get an extra clause from Jesus: "And you can show kindness to them whenever you wish" (Mark 14:7). In this reading, Jesus' words simply cannot be interpreted as any kind of attempt to draw our attention away from poverty.

Like any great teacher, Jesus had another layer of meaning to his words. Despite what I think is an unhelpful translation, the NIV contains a footnote on this phrase in Mark's gospel pointing back to Deuteronomy 15:11, which reads, "Since there will never cease to be some in need on the earth, I therefore command you, 'Open your hand to the poor and needy neighbor in your land.'" The larger context of Deuteronomy 15 describes God's vision for Jubilee, a recurring redistribution of wealth and resources to even the playing field for those who have fallen into poverty. Those listening to Jesus, themselves intimately familiar with the teachings of the Torah, could not have walked away believing that Jesus was in any way suggesting they ignore the plight of the poor.

Instead, this passage draws us to a better kind of love for the poor—one that is experienced in community. The disciples wonder whether the costly perfume they had should have been sold to give money to the poor, but Jesus reminds them that the poor should be always *with* them. Jesus is inviting them out of a mode of transactional giving and into communal solidarity. If disciples of Jesus are always among the poor, in community and communion, the needs of the poor will be recognized and met through mutual aid, rather than through the giving of money at a distance.

When the church is at its best, it celebrates community—what theologian Dietrich Bonhoeffer called "life together." Church buildings exist for the gathering of people, and programming is aimed at bringing people together. Our most sacred tradition, the Lord's Supper, is known as "communion" because of the way it is practiced together.

It's curious, then, that so many of our ministries for our unhoused neighbors look more like giveaways and assembly lines. We don't practice the presence of God this way any other time during the week. Sunday services don't look like a line down the street with parishioners waiting their turn to be prayed over before being rushed off somewhere else. We don't send members to a cafeteria counter where a pastor ladles bread and wine into your bowl and tells you to go sit down. The church is unique because everything it practices is done in community.

We are created for relationships and communities; without these, we are incomplete. Disciples of Jesus are intended to be in communion with the poor, to be "always near." Our church communities are incomplete without solidarity with the poor and marginalized in our neighborhoods. This communion resists social norms and upends economic division, enacting jubilee not as charity but as solidarity. When we can foster, come alongside, and join in community with the unhoused, God is glorified, and we are all made more whole.

FIVE

Mental Health

Disclaimer: Though I do not have any licensure or degree in mental health, psychology, or psychiatry, I have worked alongside and learned a great deal from many such professionals—though most of my experience has been learning alongside those with severe mental illness. While I trust this chapter can be helpful and illuminating on the topic, it should not be used to replace the care of a trained professional in the field, especially as it relates to your own mental health or that of someone you may know.

FOR MY SECOND interview at The Center, the executive director had me come in during drop-in hours, the busiest time of the day when close to one hundred unhoused people are on the patio drinking coffee and conversing. He only periodically asked me questions, mostly observing my comfort level as I interacted with participants—a standard interview practice for The Center.

However, my experience that day was one that most applicants don't get. Out of the corner of my eye I saw an object fly across the patio and clang against a metal railing. All conversations stopped and all eyes turned to Kelvin, a staff member and personal friend who had arranged for my interview. A flying patio chair had missed him by just a few feet, thrown by a participant named Max. Kelvin had said or done something to upset him and, after missing him with the chair, Max walked up to where Kelvin was and stared him down—his head cocked to the side in silent rage. Kelvin kept his hands to his side, turned his body slightly away from Max, and avoided direct eye contact as he repeated, "I'm not going to fight you, Max."

I would later learn these de-escalation tactics and many more from Kelvin, and I would eventually use them myself countless times. At this moment, though, I was simply in awe. After what felt like forever, with Max posturing aggressively and Kelvin remaining resolutely calm, Max turned around, walked down the street, and did not return that day.

The executive director turned to me and muttered, "Yeah, that happens sometimes. One time he had a screwdriver; that was pretty wild . . ." Then he looked down at my shirt: "OKC Thunder, huh? What do you think about Kevin Durant leaving?" The interview, and the drop-in hour, continued on as if nothing had happened.

I would later come to learn, after I got the job and eventually became Max's case manager, that he was diagnosed bipolar with aggressive tendencies. He knew this, and was forthcoming about it. His aggressive episodes were rare, but you certainly didn't want to be on the receiving end of them. Max was a passionate, thoughtful, and self-reliant person who refused to let his illness or his homelessness define him. He also loved Harry

Potter and had an annual pass to Universal Studios so that he could regularly visit Hogwarts.

While trying to navigate him into housing in LA, for which he qualified because of his mental illness, we encountered road-block after roadblock. The most disconcerting of these came when we needed to verify his mental illness for his housing application, which meant seeing a psychiatrist or psychologist to sign a form confirming his diagnosis. Having learned that he received his diagnosis at the Hollywood branch of the Department of Mental Health, I suggested we go there.

"I can't go there, I'm banned. I flipped out on them a couple times and they banned me for life."

Banned. For life. For being aggressive—a key facet of the diagnosis they themselves provided. He was restricted from getting mental health services for exhibiting the textbook signs of his mental illness. This experience, among many others, taught me the myriad ways our mental health system abandons those most in need of its services. Our system of care has glaring flaws, especially for the most vulnerable, which can cause and perpetuate homelessness.

This chapter will examine how our mental health system intersects with homelessness. The ways in which these two overlap are the topic of much debate, so it is important to dispel some myths and understand how we got where we are to see a way forward. So much of what we need in the realm of mental health requires a monumental overhaul of our systems. Since we cannot afford to wait for that even while we advocate for it, I will also recommend ways that we can improve the mental health of people experiencing homelessness here and now.

As Christians, our approach to mental health should of course be one of grace. At times, faith groups have been havens and sanctuaries for people in mental health crisis; at others, they have been antagonistic, dismissive, and inhospitable. As we have throughout the other chapters, we will be invited to see not only our complicity but also our opportunity in light of grace and all it calls us to.

Defining terms and why it matters

This chapter is broadly related to "mental health" but will often use the language of "mental illness" and even "severe mental illness." In common vernacular these terms are used arbitrarily and even interchangeably, contributing to confusion around the topic. Because of the evolving study and knowledge of the subject, and the realities of public sentiment and stigma, there isn't unanimous agreement about what each of these terms signify, even among those in the fields of psychiatry and psychology.

Here, in this book, *mental health* is a broad term encompassing everything we conceive of as psychological well-being. The Canadian Mental Health Association explains, "Mental health includes our emotions, feelings of connection to others, our thoughts and feelings, and being able to manage life's highs and lows."[1] All associated terminology, including mental illness and severe mental illness, is part of the larger scope of mental health. The "mental health care system" is the continuum of services designed to promote community mental health and serve those with mental health needs. These services can include hosting community events and activities to promote connection and decrease stigma, but also include involuntary hospitalizations for those in extreme distress.

Mental illness refers to any psychological condition of any severity. Common mental illnesses include anxiety disorder, depression, obsessive compulsive disorder, and PTSD. *Severe*

mental illness, or SMI, is a subset of these conditions, referring to disorders such as schizophrenia and bipolar disorder.
Diagnoses like depression and PTSD can also rise to the severity
of an SMI.[2] Severe mental illnesses are more often associated
with psychosis and distortions of reality, including hallucina-
tions and delusions.[3]

We all experience seasons when our mental health is better
or worse, but not all of us experience a mental illness.[4] Among
those who do have a diagnosed mental illness, very few of those
conditions—less than 6 percent—fall under the category of
SMI.[5] Mental health affects us all, but not all the same.

Differentiating these terms is crucial to understanding the
intersections of mental health and homelessness. One of the
issues we face in providing appropriate services is the breadth
that the term *mental health* encompasses. Providing mental
health services could look as simple as an elementary school
counselor doing talk-therapy with a child who's having a hard
time, or as critical as de-escalating a person wielding a knife
while experiencing a psychotic episode in a crowded shopping
center. These situations could not be more different, yet both
fall under the same umbrella of "mental health."

Why does this matter? In the past few decades, we have
seen significant progress in destigmatizing open dialogue about
mental health, and services like therapy and psychiatry are more
accessible than ever. This is the direct result of greater funding commitments to mental health at multiple levels of government. However, the quantity and quality of care for people
with SMIs has not seen much change. A remarkable amount
of good has come from increased funding for mental health
generally, but this funding rarely comes with stipulations that
it be used to serve people whose mental health needs are most

acute. For this reason, it's important to be specific in discussing mental health and homelessness: Are we advocating for broad mental health services that serve everyone, or targeted care for those whose needs are most severe? The first is a lot easier and benefits all of us, not just the most vulnerable few. But if we continue doing only the former, the most sorely in need will always be left behind.

Prioritizing the needs of the most vulnerable is always a good starting place—nevertheless, it is also true that what is good for mental health generally is good for everyone. While those with severe mental illnesses may need a very specific treatment plan with a variety of supports and interventions, everyone's mental health improves when people are provided with basic needs, both material—food, clothing, housing, healthcare— and intangible—relationship, community, sense of purpose. We should not collapse all of mental health into a one-size-fits-all methodology, but we also do not have to be specialists in the treatment of SMIs to make a direct impact on people's mental well-being. We will hold these two things in tension as we consider what role the church has to play in serving those who experience homelessness and mental illness.

Where we are and how we got here

In chapter 2, we came to understand that a lack of affordable housing is the driving cause behind homelessness, and that mental illness is one of many risk factors that contribute to someone's likelihood to experience it. We automatically associate homelessness and mental illness, sometimes because of our own anecdotal experience but more often because of stereotypical and stigmatizing portrayals in media. This serves to create distance and fear, and discourages us from asking a crucial question: *Why* does having mental illness put people at such a high risk of homelessness? When we do, we discover it wasn't always this way, and it doesn't have to remain so.

Research psychiatrist E. Fuller Torrey offers a thorough examination of the historical breakdown of mental health care in America in his book *American Psychosis*. Before 1960, mental illness was primarily addressed by large mental health institutions and asylums. At their height, these institutions housed over half a million people. Because of mounting stories of abuse as well as shifting public sentiment as a result of dramatizations like *One Flew Over the Cuckoo's Nest*, funding was obliterated for these types of institutions, and their patients were discharged.[6]

The stated goal of deinstitutionalization was to shift the care of those with mental illness to community-based outpatient centers. Unfortunately, this crucial step never fully materialized. Politicians bickered about whose responsibility it was to fund them. Community mental health centers that did receive funding capitalized on the ambiguity of the requirement and had no intention of serving those with severe mental illness. Many of the patients discharged from these institutions had nowhere to go and wound up living on the streets.

The dream of a federal commitment to community-based mental health centers was dashed, and it remains in a state of disarray to this day. We dismantled a flawed system for a vulnerable population, but have yet to put anything that comes close to matching the need in its place. For anyone whose mental illness causes them to lose income and their supportive community, there are primarily two places one can expect to end up: the streets or jail.[7] This amounts to a vast overrepresentation of severe mental illness in homelessness and incarceration: while only 6 percent of Americans suffer from severe mental illnesses, SMIs affect approximately 20 to 25 percent of the unhoused population and 15 to 20 percent of those incarcerated.[8] Our inability to conceive of and fund a robust system of care for people with mental illness has turned the streets and prisons into the final landing spot for people who are extremely ill— places that only worsen the conditions and other risk factors that landed them there in the first place.

An irrational system

In Mark 9, Jesus encounters a young boy possessed by a vicious demon that would throw the boy into harmful convulsions. Jesus' disciples, who had been empowered and charged to cast out demons, were unable to help this particular boy. They had to call on Jesus himself, who after setting the boy free, explained, "This kind can come out only through prayer" (v. 29).

Along with many Christians, I wonder whether some biblical stories of demonic possession may be describing what we now call mental illness. Regardless of whether you're sympathetic to this idea, I have often felt the disciples' dismay when it comes to people with particularly acute mental illness; I feel lost and out of my depth.

Take Adam, for example. Adam has been coming to The Center for as long as it has existed, but if you asked him how long he's been experiencing homelessness, he'll casually reply, "Oh, a couple years." If you press him, he'll agree that it's perhaps been longer, but it will quickly spiral into delusions about how he owns a lot of property in the hills that's tied up in legal matters but will be ready soon. He's been saying the same thing to me for over five years, and the more I try to help, the more he pulls away.

And he isn't lying—at least, not intentionally. Adam genuinely believes that this is all true and lives his life accordingly, remaining unhoused just "while the legal people sort everything out." Because of this, he has passed up multiple housing opportunities and a variety of long-term services—especially mental health services. "No, no, nothing like that, I don't need that. I'm not like these other crazy people."

The term for what Adam experiences is *anosognosia*. It's a symptom most commonly associated with dementia, but it is extremely common with schizophrenia and bipolar disorder as well. The term refers to a person's inability to recognize that they have mental illness. The severity of this varies and can even change over time. Adam is by far the most severe case I've experienced.

As the National Alliance on Mental Illness (NAMI) has identified, people with anosognosia are at a heightened risk for homelessness and arrest.[9] Without awareness of their mental illness and an understanding of how to live with it, people are unable to regulate their behavior or the expectations of social settings, including programs intending to help. But much of the problem is also systemic: our social safety nets meant to serve those with severe mental illness are often designed in ways that render them functionally inaccessible.

For Adam to qualify for housing because of his mental health, he would be required to acknowledge the condition that his condition precludes him from acknowledging. If we were to pursue an alternate qualification for housing, he would be flagged in the process for stating that he owns property, regardless of the fact that this isn't true. And so Adam remains stuck in a system that's supposed to serve people exactly like him but is so incomprehensible that he can't possibly navigate it. As with the disciples in Jesus' story, it feels like the only thing I can do is pray.

The temptation we all face is to resign ourselves to the complexities of mental illness and homelessness. It leads many to surrender: "You just can't help those people, they're crazy." It cynically abdicates our responsibility to care for those with mental illness in our communities—believing that whatever fate befalls them is out of our hands. In working with clients like Adam, I've cried at the realization that for some, the systemic barriers are simply too great. I've felt the disciples' despair and a temptation to give up. I've longed to be able to do what the disciples did with the convulsing boy—just hand the healing work directly to Jesus.

When I consider how to best help Adam, Max, and so many others, it isn't the mental illness alone that creates obstacles for care. The system in place to help them is often as unpredictable and irrational as the behaviors of my clients. Whether individuals are punished for exhibiting the symptoms of their illness or required to admit they have one when the illness literally prevents them from doing so, these institutions and processes are built on fundamental misunderstandings of the issues they're trying to address.

I met Steven on my first day working at The Center as I shadowed a group we held at the local library. He walked in during the middle of a discussion and immediately began talking over everyone. He wasn't yelling or being rude at all, but his energy left little room for anyone else to speak. I was the only stranger to him in the room, and he greeted everyone else by name and with a story of some kind. When it finally occurred to him that he had interrupted a group in progress, he fell to his knees, prostrating himself and kissing the ground, begging for forgiveness and insisting we continue the group, unaware that his performance of remorse was as much of a distraction as his entrance had been.

I'll never forget the day about a year later when I received some Social Security Disability paperwork in the mail for Steven. Steven is diagnosed with bipolar schizoaffective disorder, and receives around $1,000 per month through SSDI. This is more than many receive and can go quite far on the streets (even if it's nowhere near enough to afford rent).

While serving as a legitimate lifeline for so many, this program has a glaring flaw: SSDI requires individuals to recertify their disability every three years. Never mind that the program has been set up so that only those with permanent and incurable disabilities qualify. There is no known cure for schizophrenia. There is nothing that could happen to Steven that would disqualify him as a valid recipient. This was a condition of his enrollment in the first place. Yet he and every other permanently disabled recipient of this benefit have to confirm every three years that they have not been miraculously cured of their incurable ailments.

To compound the absurdity, the paperwork comes as a largely unreadable packet, full of jargon and confusing language. I had to consult with my more veteran colleagues to understand it. If I were not there to receive this mail—not a guarantee for people without a physical address—and then translate it for Steven, he would have had no way of comprehending what is required of him. As if that weren't enough, Steven had to recertify with a specific doctor he had never met, located fifteen miles away, and was given a specific date and time, as well as a warning about what would happen if he missed the appointment.

On the day of the appointment, Steven showed up not at the doctor's office fifteen miles away, but at our gate. He had completely forgotten, and his appointment was in twenty minutes; none of us was able to leave to take him there. In a last-ditch effort, I called an Uber and loaded him in the back of it. I promised the driver a generous tip and sent them down the road with a hope and a prayer. Somehow, Steven made it to the doctor's office, had the wherewithal to wait for over an hour to be seen, and was recertified. I'm still in disbelief to this day that it all worked out.

I'm not quite cynical enough to believe that this system was designed for people to fail. But I must admit that if I were in charge of creating a system that *was* designed for failure, it would look a lot like the one we have.

Working with and caring for people with severe mental illness is difficult enough without such a nonsensical system complicating every step of the process. If we made it a priority to overextend generosity in care to the most vulnerable instead of looking for any and every reason to cut it off, many of our current systems would need to undergo a dramatic change.

Trauma and recovery

We need not wait for a complete system overhaul to address the mental health needs of people experiencing homelessness within our reach. Many of the best tools at our disposal are, in fact, the very same things that we've already explored: housing, trauma-informed care, authentic relationships, and safe community. All these are innate human needs that, when met, contribute positively to mental health.

As a reminder, mental illness falls under the larger category of mental health—the two are not synonymous. A person can be diagnosed with a severe mental illness but, through managed care and stability, experience prolonged periods of good mental health. Another person could have no mental illness to speak of but experience poor mental health nonetheless because of a recent trauma, a lack of stability or resources, or any number of other causes.

Because of this, anything that promotes mental health is applicable and positive for anyone, regardless of whether they experience severe mental illness. This does not mean that everyone's mental health needs are the same, or that promoting positive mental health is a substitute for psychological or psychiatric intervention for those who need it. It simply means that we as Christians have an opportunity to make a positive impact on mental health for everyone through things that are within our scope and control. We do not need to be trained therapists or psychiatrists to improve the mental health and wellness of unhoused people we come into contact with. (Though any opportunity to collaborate or seek consultation with a professional is always a benefit.)

In identifying ways to proactively improve mental health, understanding trauma and its effects is essential. Trauma-informed care (introduced in chapter 3) provides the baseline for understanding the experiences of unhoused people, which are often characterized by trauma both past and present. When a new person first comes to The Center, I do not know whether they have a mental illness, a diagnosis, a prescription, or a therapist; but I can assume with near certainty they are living with trauma.

In her seminal work *Trauma and Recovery*, psychiatrist Judith Herman outlines five key elements on the pathway to recovery from trauma. They will sound familiar, as four of the five key elements[10] resonate with the Housing First model and trauma-informed care:

1. A healing relationship—"Recovery can take place only within the context of relationships; it cannot occur in isolation."[11] Because trauma affects our capacity for trust and autonomy, healthy and empowering relationships are key to the healing process.

2. Safety—"Survivors feel unsafe in their bodies. Their emotions and their thinking feel out of control. They also feel unsafe in relation to other people. . . . No other therapeutic work should even be attempted until a reasonable degree of safety has been achieved."[12] This safety begins with bodily safety and extends to the environment, including safe living conditions.

3. Reconnection—In this stage, survivors "take power in real-life situations," exercising autonomy in new ways that allow for a reconnection with the self as well as others.[13]

4. Commonality—The experience of community is a powerful mode of recovery: "Trauma isolates; the group re-creates a sense of belonging. Trauma shames and stigmatizes; the group bears witness and affirms. Trauma degrades the victim; the group exalts [the person]. Trauma dehumanizes the victim; the group restores [the person's] humanity."[14]

Each of these steps has as much to do with environments and forces outside of the professional therapy setting as within it. A person's ability to work through trauma, much like their ability to manage the symptoms of mental illness or poor mental health, has as much to do with their personal stability, social support, and safety as it does with the treatment they actively seek for mental health support.

Because this is true, housing has become a crucial intervention for people who experience mental illness and homelessness. Under the old model, people had to demonstrate their "readiness" for housing by complying with a particular treatment plan, which often includes attending multiple appointments, managing medication, and numerous other hoops. Asking people to comply with treatment while vulnerable on the streets is not only entirely nonsensical, but also perpetuates trauma. Housing First, on the other hand, has proven incredibly effective at stabilizing people with severe trauma and mental illness. This should come as little surprise: people with a safe place to sleep at night and a place to store medications are in a much better position to seek and maintain treatment.

Because of significant structural barriers—like those I encountered with Adam, Max, and Steven—providing housing first isn't always possible. But that doesn't mean these individuals are cut off from the possibility of recovery. It's often the case that trust has to be built with people before they are willing to accept help, especially when they've been disappointed or hurt by service providers before. It's also worth noting that three of Dr. Herman's five elements of recovery have to do with connection and community, the same topics covered in the previous two chapters. Healing relationships, reconnections, and commonality are all possible for people experiencing homelessness right now, and each can be fostered and supported by Christian communities. Creating a space where people can come, spend time, and connect with one another is an evidence-based practice for improved mental health and trauma recovery, both for unhoused folks and for the broader community.

Mental health and the church

While helpful treatments are available and individuals may experience seasons of peace, those who live with mental illness know it can periodically resurface and may never subside completely. For this reason, communities sometimes reject what they view as a burden of perpetual care and support for people who, in their eyes, will never "get better." Unfortunately, both for those with mental illness and for the community, this is only a recipe for misery.

Churches ought to be supportive communities, unwaveringly hospitable and accessible to those with mental illness. Overall, however, this has not been the case. Faith communities have been historically dismissive and ignorant of and even hostile toward the topic of mental health. Symptoms of depression and anxiety are sometimes ascribed to a shortage of faith in God. Erratic behavior is considered distracting or even ungodly. Some worship settings require stillness and quiet, sometimes to the exclusion of anyone who cannot meet such standards.

Although a proper theology of mental health is outside the scope of this book, you can tell a lot about your church's ability to navigate severe mental illness by how it talks about mental health in general. If your church struggles or outright refuses to have conversations about mental health, or to provide adequate, research-based support for those with anxiety, depression, or other more common mental health struggles, your church will certainly not be a safe place for those with more acute diagnoses like schizophrenia or bipolar disorder. If churches are antagonistic or dismissive toward depression and anxiety, they will be ill-prepared to confront more severe symptoms. As Jesus purports in Luke 16:10, "Whoever is faithful in a very little is faithful also in much; and whoever is dishonest in a very little is dishonest also in much."

In this sense, we can all start with this question for ourselves and our local church communities: Are we safe for people with mental health struggles? Do our relationships and programs provide low-barrier and consistent care for people? If your church has a program for unhoused folks, do you expel or ban people who exhibit erratic behavior? Knowing that these behaviors may not be willful, how can your program adjust to offer safety for all while also including those who require greater care and intention? If your programs are frequented by people with mental illness, are there any partnerships you can form with local nonprofits that work with this population?

Is your Sunday service a place that would welcome and hold space for someone with unregulated mental illness? If not, what would need to change?

If we truly want to end homelessness, our theologies and our ecclesiologies need to be big enough to welcome people with severe mental illness to find acceptance and support in our churches. We need to become comfortable with the idea that there is no correlation between the amount of faith someone has and their mental health. However, there *is* a direct correlation between mental health and the amount of community support a person has.

The church can be a positive force for mental health among the most vulnerable, never giving up on people as they navigate a lifetime of care management, with all its ups and downs. Grace calls the church to this most holy, sacred work: to care for the most vulnerable and sick for as long as it takes.

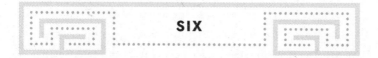

SIX

Substance Use and Overdose

JAMEEL WAS THE first person I ever knew to die of a drug overdose. It happened during my first year working at The Center. He died on a sidewalk, alone, presumed asleep and lying in the open for hours.

To be human is to strive for meaning and sensibility in death, and early in my career I was reeling to make sense of Jameel's. I found myself resorting to stereotypes and easy answers. My framework had not evolved much beyond "Drugs, and anyone who uses them, are bad!" I found myself blaming Jameel for succumbing to his addiction, angry at the prevalence of drugs on the streets, and despondent at my sense of powerlessness.

As instinctive as these responses were, I couldn't reconcile them with the reality of Jameel or the hundreds of other unhoused and addicted people I had come to know. These responses reduced Jameel—an easygoing, steadfast presence in our recovery and art groups—to a stereotypical "addict." In reaching for pat answers, I had diminished his complex situation on the streets to one that traded on my fears and resentments—themselves rooted in a lifetime of messaging, assumptions, and generalizations, internalized and echoed not just by me but by my friends, my family, the media, and even the church.

This glaring discrepancy, one that pits data and experience against my implicit beliefs, has prompted a years-long and ongoing pursuit for a more nuanced, grace-filled, and accurate understanding of substance use and addiction. I've come to recognize that our dominant narratives of addiction, often held together by myths and misconceptions, are dangerous. We have for a century built our Christian philosophy of addiction on theological ideas that corner us into moralizing drugs and the people who use them to such an extent that the only available response is judgment and punishment.

This not only prevents us from understanding the nuances of substance use and addiction but leads us to hostility and rejection as opposed to care and embrace. When it comes specifically to people who are unhoused and also use substances, our approach is all the more misguided and judgmental. Effectively and compassionately addressing substance use and addiction as experienced by our unhoused neighbors requires that we root our interventions in truth rather than faulty myths.

Focusing on the crisis

The most egregious myth pertains to the way we exaggerate the overlap between homelessness and substance use. The crisis related to substance use and homelessness is not that all unhoused people use drugs, but that those who are unhoused and *do* use are at increased risk of death compared to other drug users. As with mental illness, the data certainly show that substance use is significantly higher for those experiencing homelessness—but the relationship is more complicated than simple cause and effect. In their book *In the Midst of Plenty: Homelessness and What to Do about It*, Marybeth Shinn and Jill Khadduri make an enlightening comparison: "College students have high rates of substance use; as with homeless adults, the favored substance is alcohol. But observers rarely claim that young people become college students because of their substance use."[1]

The National Coalition for the Homeless suggests what I've experienced to be true from knowing so many unhoused people who use: homelessness causes substance use as often as, or more often than, substance use causes homelessness.[2] While it's not uncommon to hear a story of someone's addiction causing housing insecurity, the story I hear more than any other consists of people who have come to experience homelessness and only then begin using as a means of coping.[3]

Homelessness increases exposure to drug use and enhances the likelihood that someone will come to use while also heightening all the associated risks of drug use. For those who use while unhoused, the risk of incarceration for possession and use increases. Because unhoused individuals are typically using in unsafe and unsanitary conditions, and with less access to medical care, the risk of physical harms such as infection or injury is also higher. For these same reasons, the risk of overdose death for people experiencing homelessness is significantly higher as well.

We cannot hope to end homelessness without wrestling with the complexity of substance use and addiction. However, the deadly effects of use and addiction, especially for people experiencing homelessness, constitute a reality that requires our urgent attention. Understanding how to respond to the critical situation we face can reveal much about our broader cultural response to addiction and drug use, and can later inform our understanding of treatment and recovery.

Since 2013, drug overdose has been the number one cause of accidental death in America—and for people ages twenty-five to sixty-four, the number one cause of death, period.[4] While the use of a variety of different drugs (both legal and illegal) can result in a deadly overdose, the current crisis is primarily tied to opioids. Opioids are a specific class of substances that range from prescription pain relief drugs like oxycodone and hydrocodone to illegal drugs such as heroin. These substances bind to receptors in our body that trigger the release of dopamine, generating an experience of euphoria. The catch is that the same bodily systems activated by opioids are also responsible for such crucial functions as breathing. When these receptors are overloaded, breathing can depress to the extent that the brain and heart do not get enough oxygen; death typically comes in the form of asphyxiation or cardiac arrest.

Demand for opioids increased significantly in the mid-2000s, due especially to widely documented overprescription for use in pain treatment. A wave of reforms in the late 2010s culled this practice by doctors and penalized the pharmaceutical companies who instigated it, but the damage was done. Incomplete reforms meant that people whose addictions had been created and sourced by their family doctor would now be shut off with nowhere to turn but the illicit market. That market, essentially hand-delivered a windfall of new customers, quickly and eagerly adjusted its sourcing and production methods to meet demand.

Enter fentanyl. Used in hospitals for decades and about a hundred times as potent as heroin, fentanyl's entrance to the illicit market coincided with the steepest increase in overdose deaths in the past decade, a spike of over 20 percent from forty-seven thousand in 2015 to fifty-eight thousand in 2016. In 2020, overdoses accounted for eighty-one thousand lives lost.[5]

Rather than presented as one option among others, fentanyl was instead introduced as a cutting agent, grafted into opioids like heroin to increase potency and, as a result, reduce production costs. Because fentanyl is synthetic, this process can be repeated continually to meet suppliers' needs. With the proliferation of these synthetic opioids, people are overdosing not because of any change in their patterns of use, but because the substances they are putting into their bodies are increasingly—and worse, unpredictably—potent.

To make matters worse, fentanyl and its related strains—such as carfentanil, itself a hundred times more potent than standard fentanyl—are now turning up in a wide range of drugs. Stimulants like meth and cocaine are now testing positive for the presence of fentanyl. This means that people who have never used or even desired to use opioids are dying of opioid overdose without warning.

A national crisis for all of us is an absolute disaster for people experiencing homelessness—a 2016-2018 study in Los Angeles County found that overdoses kill unhoused people at a rate 26 times higher than they do those who are housed.[6]

Barry

It was 2016, the same year of the unprecedented spike in overdose deaths, that I met Barry.

Barry was a regular at The Center for more than six years and one of the most interesting people I've ever known. He cut his own mullet and would combine unique, surprising articles of clothing, like a burly scarf on a warm day or a colorful skirt with an otherwise masculine or unisex outfit—all a reflection of his individuality.

He also had an odd penchant for what I would come to call "wholesome breaking and entering." He spent one summer breaking into The Center almost every day. For a five-and-a-half-foot, portly guy, he sure could get through a window—even one on the second floor. But rather than stealing or causing damage, he mostly just wanted to play solitaire. One time he cooked spaghetti—in a deep fryer, no less—washed all his dishes, and tucked away his leftovers in the fridge (ostensibly to return to them the next day). He would make a sincere effort to leave before anyone—usually me—arrived in the morning. Perhaps it goes without saying, but he didn't always succeed.

We learned of Barry's passing on an August afternoon. Despite having been housed in another part of Los Angeles, he had been found dead of a fentanyl overdose in the streets of Hollywood.

His journey with substance use had been lifelong—years of sobriety and use interrupted by cyclical periods of relapse and recovery. He knew his boundaries, his limits, and exactly how much to take to get what he wanted out of it. How he'd died was particularly wrenching because we knew Barry's drug of choice was crack cocaine, not opioids. It's likely Barry had no clue that his familiar dose had been cut with fentanyl. He would have had no reason to anticipate the specific symptoms of an opioid overdose. All the while, fentanyl slowly stopped his breathing, and then his heart.

At Barry's memorial, we celebrated his life by eating spaghetti and, in remembrance of the only person who would ever break in with so much care, christening our newly installed alarm system in his honor. When tragedy threatens to crush our hope, we grieve deeply but also choose to celebrate the unique and wonderful life of the person we've lost. This is what allows us to recommit to the work and to our friends who remain.

This crisis is personal and urgent: our neighbors and friends living on the streets are at imminent risk of overdose as we debate how much money their lives might be worth—or if they're even worth saving at all. In Jesus' time, the analogous debate was regarding how to properly interpret the laws of the Sabbath, with many having accepted a long list of forbidden tasks meant to keep the sanctity of this day of rest. Nonconformist that he was, Jesus played it fairly loose, often drawing the ire of the local Jewish leaders. On one occasion, when Jesus was confronted about this, he responded: "If one of you has a child or an ox that has fallen into a well, will you not immediately pull it out on a sabbath day?" (Luke 14:5). His critics remained silent because when it meant saving a life (or even their livelihood), they knew, by intuition or experience, that the rules were no longer the lone priority. When it comes to saving lives, our dogma comes second.

Resurrection

By far our best life-saving medical intervention for opioid overdose is naloxone (known to many by the brand name Narcan), an opioid-reversal drug that has found an essential role in emergency services and street-based medicine. Its ability to reverse an overdose is nothing short of miraculous: naloxone bumps the opioids off the receptors and binds to them itself, allowing functions like breathing to resume almost instantly.

It's no surprise that many people of faith involved in this work have likened an overdose reversal to "resurrection," framing this life-saving intervention as an opportunity to counter death with new life. In an article for *Christianity Today* in 2017, emergency physician Lindsay Stokes called naloxone "grace in a syringe."[7] Even better, naloxone is now commonly available as an easy-to-administer nasal spray, making this small bit of grace even more accessible and user-friendly. Anyone can be trained to administer naloxone in about fifteen minutes, and in most states and provinces you can get it at a pharmacy without a prescription.

As the lives of so many in our community continued to be taken by overdose, I became a trainer myself and now teach its use to our staff at The Center. In grateful disbelief that there was such a simple and easy way to help save the lives of people I cared about, I eagerly recruited anyone I could to join me in the fight against overdose deaths. Surely the wide use of naloxone was something everyone could get behind.

Yet in June 2017, during an especially deadly season of overdoses in the Midwest, a city councilmember in Ohio devised a shocking "three strikes" policy in an effort to reduce emergency-response spending. EMTs would use naloxone to revive the same person only twice; the third time they would be instructed to let the person die.[8] Saving lives—at least these lives—was too hard on the budget.

The motion never passed. It was met with national outrage, and rightfully so. But the councilmember never recanted the idea, describing it as "out-of-the-box thinking." But the sheriff in the same county decided that his officers would no longer carry naloxone, citing similarly dubious reasoning.[9] As someone who counts as friends those who are at the highest risk of overdose, the callousness of these approaches is deeply saddening, even enraging. It may be tempting to see these realities and our responses to them as extremes, and therefore outliers, rather than examples of our ingrained beliefs pushed to their most disturbing end, our indifference and callousness holding up even in the most desperate circumstances.

How many times should we save the life of someone who is overdosing? Two? Three? I can't help but hear Peter asking Jesus how many times he ought to forgive in Matthew 18:21: "As many as seven times?" And Jesus responds, "Not seven times, but, I tell you, seventy-seven times," (Matthew 18:22) sometimes translated as "seventy *times* seven." Whether the answer is 77 or 490, the point is that we don't keep count, we simply give (and forgive) in grace. Jesus goes on in this passage to tell a story about a landowner whose debts are forgiven, but who then harasses those who owe him money. The good things God gives to us, God expects us to give to others—including the forgiveness of debts. If we believe that God's grace gives us countless chances to repent and make a new choice, who are we to put a limit on the number of times we are willing to save a life?

Since becoming a trainer, I've held dozens of trainings—anyone who would listen would get a one-hour presentation and leave with two doses of Narcan. When COVID-19 hit and virtual communication became ubiquitous, I began holding a specific, virtual version of my training for Christians hoping to save lives.

People of faith from all over the United States, Canada, and beyond have attended the online, faith-oriented version of my training to learn more about the crisis and how to respond to it. People attend for a variety of reasons: they live in communities where overdoses are increasing, serve in ministries that directly or indirectly work with people who use, or have lost someone dear and hope to prevent another such loss. It's been one of the greatest blessings of my career to help these Christians learn how to connect their faith to the opioid crisis—not with fear, shame, or judgment, but with hope, compassion, and a faith in resurrection.

Before we close the training, we recite together a blessing written by professor and theologian Sharon Fennema, which I learned from a group called Faith in Harm Reduction. I hold up the boxes that I will send out to the attendees, and we all pray, together, a benediction over the medicine itself. Part of that prayer reads:

> We know that we need each other to survive, so we ask you to bless these [naloxone] kits, and all those who will use them, and all those who will be in need of them. Make them and us instruments of resurrection, that suffering will be released, that injury will be transformed, that joy will arise, that strength will take hold, that hope will take wing, and that death will yield new life.[10]

This prayer holds the hope and posture of grace, freely received and freely given, to carry into the difficult, hope-starved realities of substance use and addiction: that we can be people of resurrection of the body and the spirit together, taking every opportunity to save the sacred lives of vulnerable people without any question of whether we think they deserve it or are worth it. Only with grace as our starting place—as our default setting—can we begin to address a situation so complex and devastating as substance use and addiction.

Matthew

An obstacle that many Christians face in being able to effectively administer naloxone is actually finding themselves in a situation where it's needed. The church's long history of shame and judgment around drug use makes it hard for drug users to trust well-meaning Christians with the truth: that they do use opioids, and may not be planning to stop anytime soon. To overcome that barrier, we Christians need to learn how to talk about drug use nonjudgmentally—to talk about it with grace. I learned the importance of this from my friend Matthew.

Matthew sat in on a Narcan training session I led with a group of formerly unhoused clients who are part of our ambassador program. Like most of the group, Matthew lives in permanent supportive housing, where many neighbors may be in the midst of active substance use and recovery. The whole group was especially engaged in the presentation, asking lots of good questions with a genuine earnestness to learn and get it right.

Matthew came back to me two days after the training, absolutely beaming. He couldn't wait to tell me: "I used that Narcan! I need some more!"

I asked what happened; the story was incredible. After the training, he went back to his apartment building and knocked on his downstairs neighbors' door. A couple lived there, who Matthew knew used heroin. He told them that he had been trained in Narcan and if they were ever in trouble, to call him.

The call came the next day. Matthew went downstairs with his Narcan and followed the steps of the training to a tee, and was able to revive his neighbor and, ultimately, save their life. After telling me this story, I gave Matthew as much Narcan as he wanted, and encouraged him to share it with the couple themselves and even teach them how to use it.

I think about this story a lot, and not simply because the timing of it feels miraculous. What is most striking to me is the way Matthew knew to go to his neighbors and tell them what he had learned, and that they called him when it was time. That part of the story wasn't spontaneous, and it doesn't feel miraculous in a traditional sense. It was the result of a history of trust, honesty, openness, and friendship. Matthew, who has never used heroin, was comfortable having open conversation with his neighbors about their drug use in a way that didn't communicate shame or disdain or lead to distrust. He cared about their lives, and they ended up trusting him with theirs.

Putting naloxone in the hands of trained and compassionate people across the country is an act of hope. It is a practice of intervention that values kindness over judgment, life over death. It is a defiance of the prevailing worldview that people who use and are addicted to drugs have forfeited their worth. It is an enactment of the belief that people like Barry and Jameel deserve to live, to be loved, and to find something like recovery in that love—if they can only live long enough to see it.

Harm reduction

The use and distribution of naloxone is one aspect of a larger, growing methodology toward substance use and addiction called "harm reduction." This phrase has been used throughout previous chapters, as it pertains to more than just substance use—the idea that we should minimize harm for people rather than insisting on perfection has wide-reaching applications. However, it is most often associated with substance use because of its application in contrast to our traditional approaches, and because it stirs up the most controversy.

"Harm reduction" is a set of beliefs for approaching substance use and addiction that highlights users' choice, autonomy, and safety. It believes that drug policy should not be about punishing people who use or trying to eradicate use altogether, but should reduce the harms that come to people and communities as a result of using drugs. An example includes offering a needle exchange, where people can turn in used needles and obtain clean ones so that when they feel compelled to use, they have safe supplies with which to do so. This method was pioneered during the AIDS crisis when activists realized that the disease was spreading through drug use, so they began illegally exchanging needles and in doing so saved many lives. Needle exchanges are now widely used and very effective, though they remain illegal in many US states.

These types of interventions often cause people, especially Christians, to bristle, but the principle of harm reduction is intrinsic to most public health policy. We know that most accidents could be avoided if traffic laws were obeyed, yet we require cars to have seatbelts and continually raise the standard of vehicle safety. We know that cigarettes cause devastating health problems, but rather than outlawing them, we restrict forms of advertising and tax them heavily to reduce their use especially among young people (and have been quite successful!). Why wouldn't we apply this tried-and-true methodology to drug policy?

Jesus, too, practices a form of harm reduction when he saves a life imminently threatened not by illness but by "justice," in John 8. The Pharisees had dragged before him a woman who was "caught in adultery," declaring that the law required them to stone her to death, and they asked what Jesus thought they should do.[11]

Rather than engage in a debate over the particular law, he instead subverted the Pharisees' entire framework: "Let anyone among you who is without sin be the first to throw a stone at her" (v. 7). Slowly but surely, everyone but Jesus walked away.

Jesus went a step further to tell the woman, "Neither do I condemn you" (v. 11). Despite being the only one who could, he still didn't. He simply told the woman to "Go your way, and from now on do not sin again." a nod to the hope that she would not again find herself in the same precarious situation, yet he offered no condemnation, and no prerequisite of a change in her behavior.

We would do well to remember the words of Paul: "God proves his love for us in that while we still were sinners Christ died for us" (Romans 5:8). At no point does the question of whether a person "deserves it" enter the equation.

When we intervene or design programs to save lives and reduce harm, we do so with the hope that healing and wholeness come next. The opportunity for change, however, comes *after* the help has been provided. Help is not dangled as a reward for change.

When grace like this is offered freely, without expectation or judgment, it can have a transformational effect. One addiction specialist calls this approach "a potent psychological intervention," a sign to that person that their life has worth even in the midst of their addiction:

> The unexpected kindness of being helped without expectations is itself a potent psychological intervention. . . . [It] opens doors to hope in surprising ways. . . . It is unconditional kindness and imbues what looks to outsiders like irredeemable ugliness with startling moments of transcendent beauty.[12]

This former addict and now advocate and journalist, in describing the approach of harm reduction, sure sounds like she's describing God's grace.

We can begin to find a way forward if we, as Dietrich Bonhoeffer wrote, "learn to regard people less in light of what they do or omit to do, and more in light of what they suffer."[13] People who use drugs and suffer addictions are not inherently worse than anyone else; and grace reminds us that we treat people based not on what we think they deserve, but on how God has commanded us to treat one another—how God has treated us.

If we start with grace, it can transform everything we believe (and do) about addiction, and it can transform the lives of those who are in desperate need of healing and wellness.

SEVEN

Addiction and Recovery

UNHOUSED PEOPLE ARE vulnerable to the worst and harshest by-products of substance use. Not all of these by-products, though, are inherent to the substances themselves. Many of the harm that comes to people who use drugs stems from how we, as a society, understand and treat people who struggle with addiction. For over a century, a few voices have dominated the conversation, especially for people of faith. These voices have provided some crucial tools in fighting addiction, but have also failed to keep up with what we've come to learn about addiction from the fields of sociology, psychology, and medicine—all of which are indispensable to effective treatment and recovery.

As we have failed to keep pace with our understanding of addiction, addictive substances themselves have been evolving in dangerous new ways. While most of our modes of treatment and care were developed in response to alcoholism, the emergence of cocaine, opioids, and methamphetamines has amplified the risk and severity of addiction. For all these reasons, we should dedicate ourselves to fully understanding addiction in all its aspects to help all those in search of recovery.

The definition that will guide our understanding is provided by the National Institute of Drug Abuse: "Addiction is defined as a chronic, relapsing brain disease that is characterized by compulsive drug seeking and use, despite negative consequences."[1]

This definition will serve as the outline for most of this chapter as we mine it for all it has to offer us. The final section is devoted to integrating the key lessons into a model for recovery that is simultaneously effective and resonant with our faith commitments—embracing the power of grace to transform our thinking and our methods and thereby transforming those who are hurting.

Chronic and relapsing

When he was sixty-one, my dad found out he had chronic high blood pressure. When he was sixty-two, he found out that his brother, sister, and mom had all had it for years. The "family diagnosis" was known to everyone but him—they all were even on the same medication! As you can imagine, my dad was a bit miffed to find out so late about this hereditary predisposition he could've been working harder to address. Before long he found himself on the same prescription.

Thankfully, I had the benefit of finding this out at twenty-nine. Approaching my thirties and with my wife and I thinking about having children, I took the news seriously. With some fits and starts, I made changes to my diet and activity to try to get ahead of it, hopeful that I wouldn't end up taking the same medication for the same problem.

Similar to addiction, high blood pressure is classified as a chronic disease, defined by the CDC as "conditions that last one year or more and require ongoing medical attention or limit activities of daily living or both."[2] As with high blood pressure, addiction has many different contributing factors: genetic and environmental ones that are completely outside our control, as well as the choices we make in terms of what we consume, what activities we pursue, and how much toxic stress is present in our lives. It may even surprise us to learn that for both high blood pressure and addiction, we know of several different treatment methodologies catered to the severity of the disease. In each, treatment and outcomes depend a lot on early intervention and commitment.

Here is where they differ: If you have high blood pressure but don't change your lifestyle, you can still get treatment with few to no questions asked. If you are addicted to a substance, most treatment methodologies offer a single option: stone-cold sobriety. If you relapse, you may be kicked out of treatment. Over two hundred thousand people are disqualified or discharged from addiction treatment for using or for related behavioral issues.

Given that addiction is defined by its chronic nature, what sense does this make? Harm reduction advocate Bill White says it this way: "We know of no other major health problem for which one is admitted for treatment and then thrown out for becoming symptomatic in the service setting. . . . If an individual could consistently exert such control, he or she would, by definition, not need addiction treatment."[3]

With any other disease, if symptoms reappear after treatment has begun, it's usually a sign to consider other treatments. Yet for some reason, when relapse occurs—a symptom, by definition—we allow ourselves to blame the patient. Too often, the patient is banned from further treatment. Can you imagine if all medicine were practiced this way?

If my dad's body hadn't responded to the first blood pressure medication, his doctor would have prescribed a new one. If I had failed to change my habits to avoid high blood pressure, my doctor would lose his license if he withheld treatment because I didn't "deserve" it. Yet this same thing happens in recovery treatment every day. Part of this stems from the way we uplift stories of miraculous recovery.

I've heard many such stories, but none were quite as spectacular as Ben's.

I met Ben when I was an intern at Penn Avenue in Oklahoma City. Twenty years prior, Ben had been addicted to crack cocaine, cigarettes, and alcohol. As he tells it, when he became a Christian he simply stopped smoking crack and drinking . . . just like that. After a year, he claims that God told him the cigarettes were "just as bad," so he quit those too. At Penn Avenue, Ben was elevated as a leader, a part-time paid staff member who oversaw the daily lunch and Saturday breakfast and held Bible studies before and after the meals.

In the world of addiction and recovery, these stories are held up in meetings and books as exemplary, even aspirational. Those who have managed to stop cold turkey and dedicate themselves to God, recovery, and service become the standard. Ben often used his story to try to inspire others to be just like him—often toeing the line between inspirational and judgmental.

We are drawn to jaw-dropping stories of 180-degree turnarounds (even when they are usually not the whole story). They validate our desire for perfection and tidy endings, even if we would rarely hold ourselves accountable to the same standards.

This perfectionist mindset is the foundation on which we have built most of our addiction treatment.

In the traditional Alcoholics Anonymous/twelve-step model—as with its evangelical offshoot, Celebrate Recovery—sobriety is an expectation and a requirement. Groups hold chip ceremonies as beautiful communal celebrations of members' sobriety. To uproarious applause, people approach the stage to receive a chip celebrating one day, five days, sixty days, even years and decades of sobriety. If you've never been to a chip ceremony, I recommend it.

I want to suggest, however, that this overemphasis on sobriety may have unintended consequences—and I want to tell you about Will.

Will has been recovering and relapsing for as long as I've known him, which is going on six years. Meth is his vice, which he holds at bay by staying busy and active and helping others. He often shows up to The Center to water the plants, trim the trees, do some landscaping—anything to bring order to the chaos he often feels. A couple of years after I met him, Will secured housing in Hollywood with our support, affording him the covetable benefit of staying plugged in to his community after the transition.

In the six years I've known him, Will has been dedicated to his sobriety, attending groups and meetings at The Center and elsewhere around the city. I've seen him through multiple periods of use and sobriety—even a two-year stretch clean and sober. It was the incident that ended his two-year streak that forever changed the way I think about sobriety models and their unintended consequences.

He had been having a particularly rough week and was out blowing off steam with some of his neighbors. His friends began smoking weed and offered for him to join. Knowing it would calm his nerves, he took a hit and enjoyed the company of his friends.

It wasn't long before guilt and shame overwhelmed him. Will became distraught at having tossed away two years of sobriety. Programs like AA and CR don't discriminate between substances or the amount—even if the risk of harm and addiction differs wildly between substances. The only valid goal is perfect sobriety.

Knowing that he had "lost" his sobriety, and that tomorrow would be day one all over again, Will used meth. Like anyone about to start a diet, Will thought, "Sobriety starts tomorrow," and went all out. It would be a while before Will got to day two.

The truth is, Will is an inspiration. His resilience to maintain recovery through hardship and multiple relapses is a testament to his strength, not his failure. His recovery is slow, quiet, and full of small victories along the way. His recovery falls in line with the definition of addiction—that it is a relapsing condition. It would be stranger if he *didn't* relapse. Yet the dominant view of recovery sees this as a monumental loss, akin to starting over at day one.

When we only hold up stories like Ben's as the only ideal, we indirectly tell Will and those like him that they're not cutting it. Seventy percent of people in recovery relapse at least once, but when our programs expect and celebrate perfection, relapses turn into despair. Supporting recovery means learning to celebrate different journeys toward recovery, whatever they look like and however long they take.

At a conference on ending homelessness I attended in 2019, a presenter said, "AA and twelve-step programs work for some people, but I have a feeling that most of the people it doesn't work for end up being our clients." My experience says she was right. This is not to demonize or dismiss these groups altogether; at the end of this chapter, I will highlight the things that these programs do exceptionally well that should continue to be modeled in any recovery program. As 1 Thessalonians 5:21 says, "Test everything; hold fast to what is good." To use a phrase ubiquitous to AA culture itself, "Take what you like, leave the rest."

A brain disease

Understanding addiction isn't exactly rocket science, but it is a bit like brain surgery.

Substances like opioids, accelerants, alcohol, and nicotine interact with the specific part of the brain associated with pain and pleasure—they make you feel good, especially if you're feeling bad. This part of the brain develops thoroughly and quickly in adolescence, meaning that young people have a physiological urge to seek pleasure. However, the part of the brain that is associated with reasoned thinking, assessing cause and effect, and long-term consequences is still in development into the late twenties. While addiction can develop among people who first use substances later in life, adolescence can be a particularly acute time for experiences and behaviors that may lead to addiction.

Adolescent brains, then, are eager to manage pain but without the benefit of a moderating "voice of reason," as if fighting with one arm behind their back. When adolescents grow up in environments where pain is prevalent—poverty, trauma, abuse, neglect—the likelihood that they will resort to negative coping methods skyrockets. To put it crudely: the brain loads the gun, but the environment fires it.

While many coping behaviors learned in adolescence are reversible in adulthood, chemical addiction can actually rewire the brain. When substances become a primary coping mechanism, the brain learns to seek that route to relief, and directly connects the feeling to the substance, literally bypassing the brain's decision-making centers. It becomes automatic, similar to driving the same way home for the thousandth time and not remembering the drive itself. People become trapped in an unbreakable cycle that has almost nothing to do with "will" or "strength" and everything to do with the literal structure of the brain during that developmental stage.

Rather than framing the conversation around young people "under the influence" of particular substances, I wonder whether we might instead think of it as young people under the influence of a traumatic environment that their developing brain is not suited to handle. Young people in distressing situations are drawn to things that make them feel good, safe, and distanced from the harm around them. In desperate situations, drugs can provide relief. With repeated use, the brain comes to rely on the substance, culminating in the creation of a habit and even dependence—what we know as addiction.

It was four years ago, but I can clearly remember Martín telling me that he was born in August 1989 in Mesa, Arizona. The reason? I was born in August 1989 in the next city over. We both wound up in Hollywood in 2017, and would meet by chance at the front door of The Center. Only, I was a full-time staff member and he was a participant. I had a home, a career, a wife, and a dog. He slept on the front steps of a nearby church, was addicted to crystal meth, and had burned nearly every bridge he'd had in the pursuit of that high.

At first glance, it would be easy to view our trajectories though a traditional framework of choice, autonomy, and success from this example. Martín and I both started from essentially the same place and ended up in opposite circumstances. In a situation like this, we are conditioned to ask what choices set us on our respective paths. But it took only a little bit of getting to know Martín's story to upend that philosophy entirely.

Martín first got high when he was seven years old. His father sold weapons and drugs out of their house, and he stashed a lot of the drugs under Martín's bed, thinking they would be safer from thieves or police. One day Martín decided to try some for himself. When his dad suddenly burst into the room, Martín thought he was in huge trouble. Instead, his dad laughed—he thought it was funny.

Our similar origins initially caused me to think, "Wow, that could have been me!" But when I hear about his life at seven years old and think back on mine—in a house owned by my loving, stably employed parents, enrolled in a well-funded school, and connected to a nurturing community—nothing could be further from the truth. The idea that it "could have been me" is rooted in the myth that we all start from the same place and are products only of the choices we make along the way. In this case, that myth glorifies me and resents Martín for things that were well outside either of our control.

Could I have tried meth? Maybe, though I don't know where I would have gotten it. The likelihood that I would have become addicted to crystal meth in adolescence is almost zero, while for Martín it was nearly assured. In so many ways, Martín was predestined to addiction. As journalist Maia Szalavitz puts it, "Addiction doesn't just appear; it unfolds."[4]

The connection between childhood trauma and substance use has been thoroughly studied. A seminal study identified what are now referred to as adverse childhood experiences (ACEs) by asking adults a series of questions about potentially traumatic experiences and the stability of their environment from ages zero to seventeen. The questions include experiences of witnessing or being subject to physical and sexual abuse, the presence of drugs in the home, and instances of incarceration and divorce. The result of this survey can then be measured against the person's current well-being.

A high score, indicating a high number of traumatic experiences and destabilizing realities, has a direct correlation to poor physical health, mental illness, and substance use in adulthood. In one study, which looked specifically at substance dependence, it was noted that "for every unit increase in the number of types of violent crime/abuse experiences, a person's odds of developing dependence on alcohol, cocaine, and/or opioids were nearly doubled."[5]

The direct connection between substance use and brain development, forged in what are for many of us unimaginable circumstances, shows us the need for grace and empathy for anyone we encounter with addiction. We must understand that people use drugs not because they are selfish and want to feel good, but because they are hurting and want to stop feeling bad.

Compulsive drug seeking and use

Acknowledging the relationship between substance use and trauma is helpful not just for understanding those who have experienced childhood trauma, but for understanding the escalation of substance use once people come to be unhoused. In addition to the addictive chemical composition of some drugs, substance use for this group can also become compulsive because it meets a particular need.

Trauma only escalates once a person begins sleeping outside. The lack of safety, security, and basic necessities afforded by homelessness is, in many ways, a constant trauma. Since people experiencing homelessness are already likely victims of traumatic environments, it is easy to see how substance use would become so appealing.

People use drugs because *they work*. If drugs didn't accomplish something, people would stop using them after the first or second try, long before addiction might take root. Knowing what drug use provides—the very real gap it fills—is crucial to understanding it.

Knowing that opioids numb pain and provide relaxation helps explain why someone experiencing homelessness might use them: perhaps they are using them to self-medicate for physical or psychological pain, to calm their nerves in a stressful environment, or to help them sleep during inclement weather. Knowing that cocaine makes you feel powerful and energized helps us see that perhaps people use it to feel confident in a world that scorns their existence, or maybe to give them enough energy to do all that they need to accomplish in a given day. Knowing that meth keeps you alert and hyper-focused gives us similar insight: someone might use to stay awake so they can protect their belongings from theft, or to focus despite a mental illness that clouds or overwhelms their mind. These substances meet genuine needs that might be otherwise unmet for people experiencing homelessness.[6]

Edgar Allen Poe said it best in describing his own addiction: "It has not been in the pursuit of pleasure that I have periled life and reputation and reason. It has been the desperate attempt to escape from torturing memories, from a sense of insupportable loneliness and a dread of some strange impending doom."[7]

Addiction is what happens to those whose minds and bodies learn a relationship between the substance and the pain. Former addict turned journalist Maia Szalavitz viscerally chronicles her early use of heroin, writing, "Every atom in my body felt calm, safe, fed, content, and, most of all, loved."[8]

Calm . . . safe . . . fed . . . content . . . loved. These basic, human, spiritual needs often go unmet among people experiencing homelessness, especially those who are addicted. The crisis of overdose deaths prompts us not only to save as many lives as possible, but also to investigate how addiction manifests in the first place. In so doing, our imaginations are reshaped from resentment and judgment to grace, and this orients us rightly to begin exploring how to help people recover.

Despite negative consequences

The last aspect of the definition of addiction stands in starkest contrast to our current response, on both an individual and a policy level. Addiction persists "despite negative consequences"—no amount or degree of punishment or ultimatums can counter an addiction. The addiction rises to the challenge, so to speak; trying to force someone into sobriety is as futile as trying to calm someone down by screaming at them. As with housing and all other services, only what is freely chosen can be effective and humane.

Nevertheless, our fundamental approach to US drug policy is punishment. In 2020, more than one million arrests were made for drug *possession alone*—that doesn't include sales.[9] The United States holds the world's largest prison population and incarcerates more of its residents than any country in the world—664 per 100,000, one-fifth of which are drug-related.[10] Once they enter the justice system, people with drug charges are sent down a quick, devastating path. Incarceration causes people to lose jobs and relationships, with many restrictions continuing even beyond release. Because addiction is "a chronic and relapsing brain disorder," and incarcerated people are often released into financial and housing instability, recidivism for drug offenders is over 60 percent.[11]

This approach to addiction infects more than just our policies. Shows like A&E's *Intervention* popularized the idea that public humiliation is a viable approach to help someone face their addiction. Addictions are met with demands and ultimatums, putting relationships on the line against an addiction that is defined by its ability to rise to the challenge. When the addiction keeps them from meeting these demands, people are excluded from social groups, essentially driven into a state of isolation and self-loathing—the very environment in which addiction thrives.

This is not to say that there is no place for setting boundaries with people you know who experience addiction. Because of the attendant harms of substance use, it may be necessary to make difficult choices as you weigh your love and ability to care for someone alongside your other obligations. You may find you need to make the choice to cut someone off, but it's important to understand that this is a choice you're making for yourself, not an intervention.

Amid all this pain and shame stands grace, once again, drawing us back and challenging us to a better way—one that affirms and patterns itself after the God who meets us in our brokenness with transforming love instead of punishing judgment. Grace is again the answer, meeting people in the midst of their brokenness and shame with acceptance and care. In the same way that addiction escalates to overcome every obstacle and punishment, I believe that recovery rises to meet every act of grace and love. We'll now turn to evidence-based practices to support recovery that further emphasize and align with these values.

The opposite of addiction

> *Even in active addiction, people can learn and change*
> *. . . whether or not they want to stop using drugs—and*
> *whether or not their choices around drug use are totally*
> *free—they can and often do make decisions that can*
> *improve their lives and health if given the opportunity.*
> —**MAIA SZALAVITZ**, The Unbroken Brain

Dan Bigg, pioneer of the field and founder of the Chicago Recovery Alliance, was known to define recovery as "any positive change."[12] In this sense, recovery looks different for everyone and is defined by a simple belief: Better is better. Tackling addiction must be about more than what we *don't* do or what *hasn't* worked. Defining recovery as "any positive change" opens up a world of treatment and opportunities for betterment in which the church should be an active participant.

Alternative goals

Once again, we return to the idea that people are themselves the experts on their own experience and therefore ought to be the drivers of their care. When we work with someone to establish their recovery goals, they may look different from the traditional "abstinence only" path. In my own work, I've come to understand goals as falling into three primary categories: (1) using less, (2) using safely, and (3) stopping use altogether.

If we believe that "better is better," we're able to support and celebrate someone who decides to use *less* than they are currently. Because addiction is marked by compulsive use, learning to respond differently to the brain's cravings takes time and practice. "I usually use every day but I didn't yesterday" is one of my favorite things to hear from a participant who struggles with addiction. Sometimes this is followed by an ashamed "I will probably use today." Rather than feeding into that dispiriting sense of shame, I try to interrupt it by celebrating the accomplishment and encouraging them, if they are going to use, to do so safely.

Using less can also mean using something less harmful. I know many people who smoke cannabis to stave off the desire to use opioids. The harms associated with marijuana are nowhere near those of opioids: it's relatively nonaddictive, carries no risk of overdose, and in many places is legal, which minimizes risks associated with acquisition and possession.

Another method for reducing opioid use is methadone. Methadone is actually an opioid, but has attributes that reduce cravings and blunt the effects of other opioids. When used effectively in partnership with a prescribing doctor, it can be a safe and effective way to minimize overdose and other attendant risks of opioid addiction. However, because it is still an opioid, and because we have learned a knee-jerk resistance to anything less than full sobriety, there is stigma toward the use of methadone and other medically assisted treatments.

Some people are unable or unwilling to alter their use of an addictive substance, but virtually everyone is willing to take steps toward minimizing harm. This can take many forms: wanting to use heroin without reusing or sharing needles, or perhaps using with others nearby to respond to crises. We do this with alcohol all the time—encouraging people to not drink and drive, even though alcoholism is a risk unto itself. This is harm reduction at its core—shifting focus from the use itself to the potential harms that can come with it. It's important to recognize and consider this "recovery," even if we wish people were willing to make a bigger change.

Of course, full sobriety is absolutely an option, and it remains the preference for most users. To be clear, it should be freely chosen among options for it to be considered a true choice. Because of the ubiquity of the sobriety model, many people struggling with addiction aren't aware of other possible paths to wellness. Of course, many do know of these other options and still choose the sobriety model. Despite accusations to the contrary, harm reduction is not antithetical to sobriety as a choice.

Recovery capital

One of the best ways to empower people on their unique paths toward recovery is to bolster their access to resources that contribute to health and wholeness. This is similar to the Housing First approach, which recognizes that when people's basic needs are met, they are better equipped to address other areas of their life. In the world of recovery, this is referred to as "recovery capital"—a way of referring to the types of resources ("capital") a person has at their disposal to aid in their recovery.

Housing, of course, is a form of recovery capital—as the Housing First principle proposes, a stable living environment allows for improvement in all other areas of life. Money, no surprise, is another. Celebrities who wish to recover from an addiction, for example, are able to access state-of-the-art in-patient recovery and detox facilities. In the same way, healthcare and health insurance are forms of recovery capital, as the level of coverage determines access to resources.

Other forms are less tangible but just as significant. For many, faith systems and sets of beliefs are a form of capital in that they may provide an individual with solace and inspiration, and sometimes a community. Social recovery capital, in the form of a supportive friend, partner, family, or other social group, is perhaps most valuable, and something from which unhoused people are often cut off. More on this below.

When working with those who have addiction, it is important to understand that a person's environment and surrounding resources often make all the difference. Successful and long-lasting interventions come from uncoerced choices made by the individuals themselves. Regardless of whether they are ready to make a choice for their betterment right now, focusing on recovery capital is a way to minimize harm and set people up for success if and when they want to take that next step.

Connection

In the 1970s, Dr. Bruce Alexander performed an experiment that has incredible implications for recovery from addiction.[13] Prior to Alexander, researchers had conducted an experiment where they would put a rat in a cage with access to two water bottles—one with plain water, the other laced with cocaine. Over time, the rats would develop a preference for the drug-laced water, returning to it compulsively until they would eventually overdose and die.

Dr. Alexander hypothesized that the environment itself might be a significant factor, and so he created what he called Rat Park: a larger enclosure with tubing and toys for play and other rats for socialization, and then provided the same two water bottles. In this environment, the results were wildly different. The rats rarely chose the drug-laced water, and when they did, they rarely returned to it. Perhaps most significantly, there were *zero* overdoses.

This study demonstrated a key insight into recovery: relationships and community are one of the most powerful tools we have in preventing and overcoming the disease of addiction. As journalist Johann Hari concluded from his extensive work in this field, "The opposite of addiction isn't sobriety. It's connection."[14]

We must consider again our traditional approach to addiction in light of this study. We know that isolating rats in cages with access to drugs causes despair and ultimately death—yet our primary response to addiction is still to disown, abandon, and punish people (putting them in *literal* cages) for a condition best treated in community.

While we may be far from being able to re-create the utopia of Rat Park for us all, we can still build on its insights. Remembering Judith Herman's key elements for healing from trauma—the power of healing relationships, safety, reconnection, and commonality—we recognize that surrounding people with supportive, nonjudgmental communities may be the best tool we have for grappling with addiction.

To their credit, AA, the Twelve Steps, and Celebrate Recovery have been practicing the power of connection for as long as they've been around. Meetings are central to these programs, providing a space where people can listen and learn from one another and practice the steps of recovery together. Mentors who are further along in their sobriety work with newer members. Some of the steps themselves encourage reconnection to past relationships, inviting the possibility for healing and, perhaps, reconnection. While I remain critical of their curricula, these programs have always understood the value of community and connection when it comes to healing.

Understanding addiction as we redefine recovery offers us a chance at walking with the afflicted, equipped with best practices in our minds and grace in our hearts. It doesn't make it any easier—addiction remains a complex and taxing reality of our world. So few of us have been immune to its effects on our families, friendships, and communities.

But in the midst of so much pain, there is immense reason to hope. Rather than an inscrutable maze of pain and despair, addiction is both intelligible and treatable. We can unlearn our proclivity to look down on people struggling with addiction as morally inferior and see them instead as people living with a disease, often with trauma at its center. We can unlearn our impulse to punish and incarcerate our way out of the addiction crisis, knowing that it only makes things worse and that it damages our loved ones and our communities. We can learn the way of grace that embraces and welcomes those who are hurting with personalized care, nonjudgmental support, and a network of love. We can encourage one another through every pitfall, and cheer along with every change for the better.

As we've seen so often along the way, the church is positioned and sanctioned with everything it needs to be a champion of recovery. It will require us to let go of our need to inflict shame and punishment on those who use drugs, even when their using causes communal and relational pain. As much as I hope to communicate that the lessons of recovery are simple, I also recognize they are not easy. In these situations I hold Paul's words in Romans 5:20 closely, that "where sin increased, grace abounded all the more."

EIGHT

Abundance, Beauty, and Celebration

WORKING IN THE field of homelessness, it is easy to fall into a mindset of scarcity, to see only tragedy, ugliness, and pain, and to live in a constant state of exasperation. The sheer amount of need relative to available resources—housing, treatment beds, jobs, benefits—can leave us fighting over what are essentially the table scraps of the privileged. Sitting with so much unnecessary suffering takes its toll: resentment, secondary trauma, even rage. Many days I find myself battling the temptation to surrender to despair.

There are plenty of reasons for allies, advocates, and activists to lose heart, yet when I take the time to actually be with people experiencing homelessness, it's hard to stay hopeless for long. Unhoused people, especially those who have been so for years, have fought for a meaningful and beautiful life in the middle of impossible circumstances. I can't be in their presence for long without catching some of their infectious laughter, joy, and hope.

Even as my work has become increasingly administrative and supervisory over the years, the despair still creeps in. When it does, I treat it as a reminder to step away from my emails and my meetings and return to the relational, communal aspects that first brought me to the work and have sustained me throughout. I remind myself of what we reflected on in chapter 1: That if, as Jesus said, "whatever you do for the least of these you have done for me," then spending time with the unhoused and the poor is spending time with Jesus. When this is done without hurry and without a need to fix or achieve anything, God is near and hope is renewed.

In the spirit of such renewal, it is important that we reflect on the counterintuitive ways that abundance, beauty, and celebration manifest (and can be cultivated) in the midst of homelessness. In response to those who often ask me, "How do you keep going in this work?" I offer the following observations and stories. This chapter is rooted in a theological belief that God is especially present with those who are suffering, and that God became incarnate in a broken world and announced grace in spite of it. We believe in this God by listening to the voices of the unhoused, and in so doing we can hold both despair and hope simultaneously—the former to push us to action and the latter to sustain us for the long haul.

Scarcity and abundance

One of my favorite gospel stories is Jesus turning water into wine in John 2. While Jesus is at a wedding celebration, the wine runs out. Jesus has the servants fill all the reservoirs to the absolute brim with water, but when they draw it out, it has become wine—around 150 gallons of water miraculously transformed, the text tells us. And not just any wine—when the chief steward tastes it, he remarks that it is even better than the wine they had previously. And so goes Jesus' first "sign and wonder" in the gospel of John.

His later works will provide food to the hungry, healing to the sick, and even raise the dead, but early in John's gospel we find Jesus inconspicuously contributing to a celebration. This miracle used to stand out to me as peculiar, almost quaint. After years working directly with people experiencing homelessness, though, I now see it as the first of Jesus' many miracles that are loaded with significance and symbolic meaning, meant to teach us something crucial about who he is and what he came to show us.

The John 2 passage gives us our first example of Jesus' extraordinary provision, which reverberates throughout the rest of his ministry. Whenever there was not enough, Jesus provided in excess. Not enough wine for the celebration? Check again. The crowds are hungry? Jesus multiplies bread and fish until there are basketfuls left over! Jesus declares "more than enough, and better than you imagined." In a word, Jesus practiced abundance. One of my favorite biblical scholars describes Jesus' ministry in this way: "Filled with God's generosity, Jesus went around to people suffering from scarcity—of health, of acceptance, of power, of understanding—and replaced it with a gift of abundance."[1]

At The Center, we choose to give the gift of abundance on a daily basis. The linchpin of our programming is Coffee Hour, a daily opportunity for us to simply open our gates for people to enter, drink coffee on the house, and facilitate connection. Even after so many years, I still marvel as I watch our space transform demeanors, postures, and body language. It's as if the threshold of our front gate transports people from exhaustion, danger, and loneliness to rest, safety, and friendship.

Rather than focusing on what are generally considered fundamental human needs, coffee is our central offering. It is both a luxury and a basic staple, occupying a cultural gray area—ubiquitous, but not quite a necessity. Most homes contain a coffee maker of some kind, many even having multiple options ranging from an automatic Keurig to a manual pourover. Coffee shops adorn metropolitan streets, sometimes multiple in a single block with little fear of oversaturation; customers gladly pay five dollars or more for a single cup. Then there are the countless places you can get coffee that aren't traditional coffeehouses: gas stations, fast-food restaurants, even vending machines. Nonetheless, coffee is far from essential; to miss your morning coffee is, at worst, a recipe for a minor headache.

To give away for free something normally thought of as a luxury is to take a posture of abundance. It is an audacious, biblical truth to an unbelieving world: You deserve more than mere survival. Your humanity amounts to more than the sum of your basic needs. Our culture and even our churches, so accustomed to evaluating a person's worth by the amount of wealth they have or can produce, largely yield to the myth of scarcity—that there isn't enough, and we therefore need to hoard our resources and reserve luxuries for only the most deserving. But Jesus preached the gospel of abundance. When we give away luxuries to the poor—to the "undeserving"—we are preaching the gospel.

Avocado toast

In 2016, avocado toast trended on social media. An op-ed published in *The Australian* pointed to millennials' taste for the popular treat as a prime example of the generation's foolish spending habits, clearly to blame for their difficulty affording such things as a down payment on a home. It is yet another form of the pernicious belief that people deserve their poverty. The argument trickles down: If millennials can't buy a home because they waste money on toast, what irresponsible choices keep people experiencing homelessness from affording rent?

Ironically, around this time I began baking bread as a hobby. I was struck by the process: mixing basic, inexpensive ingredients—water, flour, salt, a bit of sweetener—and watching them expand (literally) into something that has satisfied hungry people for millennia.

My interest was, in part, fueled by my love of the feeding of the five thousand. (A print from a centuries-old illustrated Bible featuring this miracle hangs in my apartment.) This story is especially rich in the way that it harks back to Exodus 16, where God provides the Israelites manna in the wilderness. The manna is described as tasting like "wafers made with honey" (v. 31), a detail I find especially endearing. Reminiscent of how Jesus' wine was even better than the "good wine," this highlights for me a key aspect of God's gifts in these passages. I imagine God kneading the dough of the manna, mixing up batches and generously adding honey not to meet the Israelites' nutritional requirements, but because God desired for them to enjoy it.

The same week that the avocado toast op-ed trended across social media, I was tasked with providing breakfast for Women's Day. As I noted earlier, each Friday, The Center's drop-in program is open only to women, to create a safer atmosphere and more specialized care for a population that often does not seek out services at the same rate as men. To welcome as many women as we can, we have a special breakfast each week, which at the time was prepared on rotation by our staff members. It was my turn that week, and I knew just what to make.

That Friday, we celebrated God's abundance while eating avocado toast, laughing, and drinking—you guessed it—coffee. Seventeen unhoused women in Hollywood ate avocado toast: made-from-scratch bread pan-toasted in butter and topped with smashed avocado, bacon, a fried egg, and chili-lime seasoning.

This gesture did not open the heavens. Our toast party didn't go viral, and the stomachs it filled would go hungry just a few hours later. But then, neither did the changing of water to wine or multiplying the loaves and fishes. The party ended; the crowd dispersed. Nonetheless, these demonstrations point to what God is like and anticipate the world God desires and promises is coming. Some of the best work I've been part of at The Center has been rooted in the belief that, as Brueggemann says, "if you share your bread with the neighbor, the world will be made new."[2]

As we've spent so much time exploring, part of gospel work is reimagining how resources and power are structured, as well as our role in them. Until that reimagination takes place on a larger scale, I continue to find solace in celebrating abundance amid a culture of scarcity. To practice abundance prophetically declares there is more than enough for everyone not just to live, but to flourish. There is more than enough manna, and it's sweet. There is more than enough wine, and it's the good stuff. The writer of John, who thoughtfully chronicled this story of the wedding, would later (in John 10:10) record Jesus saying that he had come so that we "may have life, and have it *abundantly*" (emphasis mine).

Beauty

Homelessness and beauty are rarely coupled in our minds. When picturing an unhoused person, you're likely to think of someone who appears unkempt and dirty. You're also likely to picture that person looking unhappy, maybe even miserable. In your imagination, you may even be literally looking down on them as they are hunched over, seated, or lying on the sidewalk.

This isn't just our ignorant imaginations at work here, but the result of patterns in how homelessness is depicted. Media and nonprofits are frequently guilty of depicting conditions of poverty and homelessness in this way to garner sympathy and drive up donations. It is so common that it has been dubbed "poverty porn," highlighting the provocative and voyeuristic view it affords and the visceral reflexes it triggers in us.

While it may increase donations and views, it has a lasting and damaging effect on our imaginations, perpetuating stereotypes of unhoused people as separate from and lesser than. Rather than being shown people with full lives, hopes, and personalities, we are shown charity cases. It stirs our emotions to give, but not our souls to move. Writer Chanju Mwanza articulates this beautifully: "Poverty porn strips away the voice from the local communities that live in poverty. For real sustainable change to happen, we need to give these populations a real voice and present the complex nature of poverty. We need to be creating more advocates not donors."[3]

When people walk into The Center, they are greeted with close-up portraits of three of our participants, each image the size of a large poster. The photos capture them smiling, laughing, posing proudly for the camera. Rather than using people to play-act roles that reinforce "us and them" categorization, the camera can just as well be a means of capturing the inherent dignity and worth of those we too often consider undignified and worthless. In displaying these images, we offer our staff, our guests, and even our participants themselves the chance to confront that instinct and replace it with a new one.

We must be careful that our depictions of poverty minimize neither the realities of suffering nor the people who experience it. The ends of greater fundraising sums and wider awareness do not justify these means. Media and fundraising should be used not to guilt people through manipulation, but to draw our awareness to the beauty and wholeness of our fellow children of God shining through in the midst of their marginalization.

Because of our failure to perceive beauty among the unhoused, we are often satisfied with banishing services to dysfunctional and dingy facilities. Having visited many shelters and other service providers over the years, it's not hard for me to understand why unhoused people can be turned off to these resources. When it comes to service provision, we comfort ourselves by saying, "It's better than nothing!"—letting ourselves off the hook for having a space that doesn't reflect the dignity of the people we welcome into it.

Churches are guilty of this too. We are often willing to let compassionate ministries into the rec room, but rarely the sanctuary. We tolerate disrepair, poor design, and even safety and sanitation issues in ways we would never for our corporate worship or children's ministry. These are the silent ways that churches communicate what—and whom—they consider most valuable and worthy.

Embracing the abundance and generosity of God, we ought to arrange and design service facilities where people actually want to spend time. Demonstrate in your facilities budget that the missional ministries of your church matter. We have the opportunity to put our money where our mouth is—where God's heart is.

Yes, this includes larger expenses, such as restoring the facilities, fixing the air conditioning, and painting the walls. Believe me when I say I'm keenly aware of the plight of operating services on a minimal budget. Nonetheless, there are creative opportunities to instill and elicit beauty in any space. Bring in plants and art, or better yet, *grow* plants and *make* art together.

Henry, one of our most prolific artists, loves to take any new staff member or volunteer on a tour of the building, always careful to point out all his pieces adorning our walls. Currently, our Women's Day participants each have a small pot of flowers that they can return to water each week. We accomplish beauty and community simultaneously, reminding us all that the space is ours as a community. Churches especially should be places where the entire community feels a sense of ownership and participation.

We have been conditioned to think of homelessness as intolerable and unseemly, perpetuating stereotypes that keep people at a distance. We can instead choose to see beauty: people made in the image of God, reflecting that image back despite injustice and pain. And in the spaces where we hold services and hope to foster community, we can make intentional decisions to allow that image to be reflected back once more.

Everyone deserves a party

Jesus frequently spoke of celebrations in his teachings, especially through parables. As a practicing first-century Jew, Jesus was part of a culture with many annual feasts, festivals, and celebrations, and they serve as context for much of the Gospels.

The truth is, every community has "parties." Sociologists such as Ray Browne and Michael Marsden suggest that celebration is as universal to every culture as language, arguing that "all societies are 'cultures of celebration.'"[4] Religious groups have holy days, some jovial and others somber. Sports teams toast victories. Families celebrate birthdays and couples' anniversaries. Nations memorialize their heroes. Any group that could be considered a community shares the objective to simply gather and connect, sharing and reliving collective experiences and histories and imagining futures together.

Jesus was often at his most controversial and unpredictable when at celebrations and gatherings. You might find him eating dinner at the house of someone who was considered a traitor to his people, or accepting eyebrow-raising invitations from unwed sisters. On one such occasion, recorded in Luke 14, Jesus gives one of those teachings that we would much rather take figuratively. Preaching to a group of Pharisees who had invited him over, he posited:

> When you give a luncheon or a dinner, do not invite your friends or your brothers or your relatives or rich neighbors, in case they may invite you in return, and you would be repaid. But when you give a banquet, invite the poor, the crippled, the lame, and the blind. And you will be blessed, because they cannot repay you, for you will be repaid at the resurrection of the righteous. (vv. 12–14)

So when The Center moved back into its newly renovated building in 2016 and held a fancy soiree for board members, donors, and community stakeholders but not our participants, something felt incomplete. After all, our mission has always been to create community among the most vulnerable, the isolated, the outcast, and we had just had such a fun and exciting time without the community that makes us who we are.

We had another party to throw.

And so we did. The event that has come to be known as Everyone Deserves a Party remains an annual tradition. We've hired taco carts, baked pizzas from scratch out of our kitchen, set up tables for games and art. One year we had a live band, and another year we made a dance floor. Hundreds of people attend, many experiencing The Center for the first time (and what an introduction!).

The joy and playfulness that emerges captures the spirit of new creation invoked by Jesus' life and teaching. To intentionally celebrate the poor is to defy the logic of our world that divides those deserving of joy and those deserving of misery. It rehearses the logic of God that the world has been turned upside down; that "blessed are the poor."

Every year, with joyful music, tasty treats, and huge grins, we proclaim that even those who suffer greatly have reason to celebrate and be celebrated. For me, this has always carried a theological weight. The Old Testament prophets implored their hearers to believe that God could be found making a great feast among those who were hurting and suffering, which proclaimed not just that God was with them, but that their suffering would not last. In that sense, because of God, the greatest joys and deepest sufferings occupy the same space, but only one lasts.

Allen

On what would be our fourth annual celebration in 2019, this tension between joy and sorrow was at its most palpable. To this day we can't explain why, but that year saw the deaths of so many beloved members of our community; some who finally succumbed to long-term ailments, others who passed suddenly and unexpectedly, one as young as thirty-eight. We would still be mourning one loss when we would hear news of another; planning one memorial only to have to begin planning the next. We eventually had to surrender to the weight of it, deciding to hold one "Day of Remembrance" at the end of the year for all those who passed, unable to keep up with memorials for each individual.

The passing that rocked our community the hardest was Allen's. Allen was a beacon of positivity and energy—constantly smiling, welcoming people, giving out free cigarettes, and repeating the same old hackneyed jokes. Everyone noticed and most enjoyed it, even if sometimes it was just a *bit* too much too early in the morning. He always wanted to be famous in Hollywood, and among our community, he was famous for his joviality and compassion. Thank God, because he wanted to be famous for comedy and his jokes were just awful.

At our annual party he was our chief greeter, first to the dance floor, and last to leave. He's seemingly in every group picture from every year, even the ones that were supposed to be for staff only. His daily commitment to joy found its perfect arena at our celebration. For three consecutive years, he was the life of the party.

Even though Allen was one of the first people The Center ever housed, his commitment and kindheartedness brought him back to The Center nearly every day without fail for more than four years. He was a pioneer in that way, as our community would continue to be a haven to people for whom a sense of isolation continued even after homelessness had ended. He cared deeply about everyone at The Center, especially those who, like him, returned to apartments each night. One woman, who constantly struggles to maintain her housing because her placement doesn't meet all her needs, received a call from Allen every morning for two years to say hello, offer support, and assure her that everything was okay.

So when he disappeared for two weeks in 2019 and his phone gave a busy signal, we knew deep down that something was very wrong. We had already filed a missing person report and the police had been unable to make contact. It was now the day before Everyone Deserves a Party 2019, and Allen was all we could think about while finalizing arrangements and decorating our patio. We couldn't stand not knowing where our friend was or what had happened to him, so my boss Rudy and I decided that we were going to find answers.

We arrived at Allen's single-story apartment complex that surrounded an overgrown courtyard. Allen's was the first apartment on the left. Two doors, one wrought iron and another dead-bolted and heavy, prevented our entry. The windows were barred and the blinds shut, offering no view or hope of access.

I called the property manager to ask whether she had heard from Allen. She hadn't, and she noted that he hadn't paid rent the previous week—his first-ever missed payment.

We returned to the parked car to make a game plan. The property manager had agreed to come out and open Allen's unit—she was worried too—but wouldn't be able to arrive for another four hours. We called the police to see whether we had enough cause for them to force entry, but they were understandably reluctant. We decided to get some lunch—as if we could eat—and return for the property manager. I started sulking back to the passenger door when Rudy spoke.

"Hang on."

He pointed to a tiny window, about seven feet up and facing the street, positioned directly above Allen's kitchen. Rudy stepped over a tiny garden fence and stacked three stray cinder blocks one on top of the other so he could reach the window and look inside the small studio unit.

I'll never forget the sound Rudy made. "There's a corpse in there." It was a guttural whine that contained despair, disappointment, anger and said "I knew it" and "I can't believe this" all at once. Whenever that day haunts me, and I imagine it will for a long time, it's Rudy's cry that reverberates in my head—more than the image of Allen's decomposing foot visible after I climbed up, having to see for myself; more than the stinging smell of death that poured out when the firefighters finally broke down his door.

I had never before, nor have I since, had to encounter the death of a participant firsthand. I pray that I never have to again. Nonetheless, I had a realization while I sat on that curb: if Allen hadn't loved The Center so much, and The Center hadn't loved him too, he probably would've been found by the property manager wondering, despite her concern for Allen, where rent was. I thank God he was found by loving friends.

As the authorities concluded their work, we left, defeated. Rudy bought me coffee in Chinatown and an overlarge French dip sandwich at a deli in Echo Park. In many ways we were stalling, driving to random parts of the city for various items, not wanting to face our colleagues, who were just now being given the news by our executive director as they decorated for the party. They were given the choice to go home or to stay—whatever they needed.

When Rudy and I finally returned, most everyone had stayed. We huddled together, ready to deliberate: What were we going to do about the party? It took all of about thirty seconds. It was going to be hard, but we all knew that Allen would only want it one way—the party *had* to go on. Rather than pushing through the pain, though, we all called it a day so we could tap into the courage and resilience it would require to come back and celebrate in the morning.

The next day I arrived a couple of hours early to give us a head start. The team trickled in, somber but determined. We decided not to tell all the partygoers about Allen—not yet. But we knew we had to tell a few of his closest friends—we couldn't *not* tell them. Of the two people we told, one left and one stayed. The one who stayed at least knew they weren't alone in trying to hold grief and celebration together in a single moment.

Holding the tension of so much fun and celebration alongside pain and grief made the party, for me, a deeply spiritual experience. It was a microcosm of what the party itself stands for: a celebration of God's abundance in defiance of all the forces of death and despair.

Isaiah 25 understands this tension, and frames it in cosmic terms:

O Lord, you are my God;
    I will exalt you, I will praise your name;
for you have done wonderful things,
    plans formed of old, faithful and sure. . . .
For you have been a refuge to the poor,
    a refuge to the needy in their distress,
    a shelter from the rainstorm and a shade from the heat. . . .

On this mountain the Lord of hosts will make for all peoples
    a feast of rich food, a feast of well-aged wines,
    of rich food filled with marrow, of well-aged wines
        strained clear.
And he will destroy on this mountain

> the shroud that is cast over all peoples,
> the sheet that is spread over all nations;
> he will swallow up death forever.
> Then the Lord GOD will wipe away the tears from all faces,
> and the disgrace of his people he will take away from
> all the earth,
> for the LORD has spoken.
> It will be said on that day,
> Lo, this is our God; we have waited for him, so that he
> might save us.
> This is the LORD for whom we have waited;
> let us be glad and rejoice in his salvation.
> (Isaiah 25:1, 4, 6–9)

At the party that day, the day after we found Allen, I think we experienced something like what Isaiah describes. We feasted and celebrated while allowing the shroud of grief and rejoicing and gladness alike to well up and spill over from within us. I never once stopped thinking about Allen or the events of the previous day. But the party became a harrowing and hallowed place where my pain was met measure for measure by joy—the joy of the God who is a refuge to the poor and the needy in distress.

I've come to believe that a space so sacred can be found only when we draw so near to the poor that their pains become ours and their joy becomes our great mission and most cherished reward. That's what it's going to be like when God makes all things new—and while we hope and wait for that time, we can see glimpses of that mountain through the fog when we choose to celebrate God's abundance here and now.

CONCLUSION

IN AN UNDERGRADUATE preaching course, my professor taught us to approach a biblical text with the right set of questions. Generally, we tend to look at a passage wondering what it has to say to us. We want the Bible to be prescriptive, giving us life lessons and direct, applicable instruction. My professor insisted that the Bible is actually first and foremost concerned with who God is. With that in mind, he suggested we read a text in light of these questions: Who is God in this text? and How are we called to respond in light of that?

As an example, he walked us through the parable of the sower from Luke 8:

> "A sower went out to sow his seed; and as he sowed, some fell on the path and was trampled on, and the birds of the air ate it up. Some fell on the rock; and as it grew up, it withered for lack of moisture. Some fell among thorns, and the thorns grew with it and choked it. Some fell into good soil, and when it grew, it produced a hundredfold." As he said this, he called out, "Let anyone with ears to hear listen!" (vv. 5–8)

As a preacher, the easy (and typical) version of this sermon is "What kind of soil are you?" It leans right into our impulses to categorize and judge. Never mind that the soils are not active characters in the story. They simply are what they are, byproducts of their environment over which they have no control. Yet I've heard countless sermons on this text asking what kind of soil I am and what kind I want to be.

If we change the primary question as Dr. Green taught, an entirely new image emerges. Who is God in this passage? Most would say that God is the sower, and that's where this story gets interesting: God the Sower sows seeds on every soil. Astute farmers prefer to not waste good seeds, and intentionally sow where they know the soil is good and healthy and will be fruitful. God the Sower is not concerned with this, but scatters seed on every kind of soil and waits in anticipation to see what will happen. Like children raised in unhealthy environments, bad soil doesn't choose to be bad, it just hasn't been properly nurtured. Nonetheless, God the Sower offers it good seed, the same as every soil, and the opportunity to make something out of it.

How are we called to respond, given that God is like this? That is the central question I have tried to address in this book. If God is a God of grace who offers salvation, joy, and flourishing to all despite what we have done and what has been done to us, how are we called to respond to the crisis of homelessness?

I believe we are called to emulate God in the dispersal of love, care, acceptance, and resources beyond any of our misguided, moralistic categorizations—good, bad, poor, "crazy," "addict," "service resistant," "homeless by choice," "ungrateful." We are called to emulate God in abandoning these labels and giving both tangible and intangible resources generously and in abundance to all, especially the most vulnerable.

ꀸꀸꀸꀸꀸ

While writing this book, a new sort of urgency emerged that has influenced how and why I write. I began writing the book in January 2020 and finished writing the final pieces in March 2022. These two years grappling with the COVID-19 pandemic have exposed so much of the faulty wiring that powers our social, political, and economic systems. The result has been a drastic reshaping of the landscape of homelessness, albeit in unexpected ways. As we move to return to normalcy and make sweeping changes, the aftermath of the pandemic has led to a spreading national movement in the wrong direction on homelessness policy.

When the pandemic began, advocates were concerned about how it would affect the unhoused population. With life expectancies low and chronic health conditions already high, we worried that COVID-19 would wreak havoc on the streets. We were surprised when, by and large, it didn't.[1] Living primarily outdoors and isolated has been an ironic advantage against a disease that spreads more easily indoors and in close contact.

Unfortunately, while the virus itself has not spread as widely in these communities, the effects of the pandemic have been devastating. As the world closed down to prevent the virus's spread, the lack of infrastructure accessible to the most vulnerable was more glaring than ever. Resources run by churches and volunteer groups quickly dried up; public spaces like libraries and parks were closed; nonprofit employees experienced burnout and service providers became understaffed at an even faster rate than before, leading to inconsistent service delivery.

The results have been catastrophic. While we don't have data to confirm whether there is more or less homelessness overall,[2] we have seen the conditions of people on the streets worsen exponentially. While unhoused folks may not be getting sick from COVID-19 at disproportionate rates, reduced access to hygienic facilities and healthcare has had major ramifications on health and wellness. Isolation has escalated the symptoms of mental illness, and people I've seen capably managing their mental health are now more dysregulated and unstable than they have been in years. The increase in overdose deaths has drastically exceeded the normal year-over-year increase.[3]

The takeaway here is not that the world shouldn't have shut down. Instead, we should recognize from this that an entire segment of our population can't rely solely on the goodwill and charity of others for survival. While I support and encourage the involvement of churches and volunteer groups in working with the unhoused, the pandemic has exposed how untenable this is as our primary response to homelessness. Never have I been less convinced by the common argument "It's the church's job to help the poor, not the government's." The church can provide intangible resources like community and spiritual care, but the church is not equipped to function as a safety net for basic necessities for all.

In the wake of COVID-19, alarming new measures and policies around homelessness are emerging. In major cities up and down the country's coasts, drastic measures to remove unhoused people from the streets are being considered and proposed by major candidates. In Los Angeles, a current councilmember and mayoral candidate plans to build mass emergency shelters and require unhoused people to utilize them under threat of arrest.[4] The current mayor of Portland similarly suggested building three mega-shelters—each with a maximum occupancy of one thousand residents—supervised by the National Guard, and a subsequent ban on street camping.[5]

This trend is surfacing across the United States, and I fear it will only get worse. It is often wrapped in the language of compassion and empathy, but is in actuality an effort to hide the problem of homelessness instead of addressing it.[6] Laws are even being enacted to target groups offering basic needs to unhoused people. The city of Brookings, Oregon, passed an ordinance to restrict churches to offering free meals only twice a week,[7] and a month later, Newark, New Jersey, announced its own ordinance to require permits for distributing food in public.[8]

I tell you all this because I believe the practices and lessons in this book are more urgent now than when I began writing it. Before the pandemic, I (perhaps naively) believed that we were making progress and getting closer to ending homelessness. I now fear that we are headed backward, and without significant interventions we will find ourselves with a larger and more unmanageable homelessness crisis than we've ever encountered.

In this worsening reality, Christians have an opportunity to join with the vulnerable and oppose these forces of criminalization and abandonment. It is past time for us to get into some holy trouble on behalf of the unhoused. St. Timothy's Episcopal Church of Brookings, Oregon, is suing the city for the ban on meal service (and continues to serve six days a week in defiance of it).[9] Our faith demands we stand with people experiencing homelessness and advocate against solutions proposed by cities who "are like whitewashed tombs, which on the outside look beautiful, but inside they are full of the bones of the dead and of all kinds of filth" (Matthew 23:27). We must push for solutions that actually *end* homelessness, rather than ones that simply push it out of sight and out of mind.

🔰🔰🔰🔰🔰

In my second job interview at The Center, our executive director asked me a question that I find poignant even to this day: "How would you feel if someone who you meet on your first day is still in the exact same place and situation two, five, or even ten years from now? Would you be able to handle that?"

This question gets at something we must all come to terms with: Even though homelessness is resolvable—and I hold out hope that with God's help it is—not everyone we work with will find permanent housing along the way. Some will pass away long before they should. Some will fall out of the housing they worked so hard to get. Some will be so deep in the throes of addiction and mental illness that they will be unable to receive the level of care they deserve (and may even desperately want).

There are days when I liken my work to that of a doctor; swearing an oath to keep people alive while knowing that everyone eventually dies. The joy and success isn't always in defeating death, sometimes it is simply in delaying it. Knowing the toll that homelessness has on people, I've learned that sometimes, success looks more like being part of a community that knows their names, notices when they're not around, and will mourn when they pass.

In fact, I've learned that when someone is in the exact same place after five years, it may even be cause for celebration. That means the person stayed connected—stayed alive! In a world that is arranged to discard and forget the most vulnerable, survival is not a given—and resiliency is a miracle.

When we are met with these less-than-ideal scenarios, we are faced with a choice. We can become disenchanted and resentful, believing that the person themself failed and that there is just no point in trying. We can declare the problem unsolvable, and begin ignoring it once more. The other option is the one grace calls us to: To die to ourselves—our saviorism, our expectations, our design of what success looks like—and keep going. Grace means we never give up on our neighbors, just as God never gives up on us.

ꓓꓓꓓꓓ

When we lived in Pasadena, Naomi and I would take our dog, Bear, on two walks a day. The neighborhood was large, walkable, and incredibly diverse because of its (relative) affordability. We met lots of our neighbors this way, including an artist named Robert.

Robert would stop us on our walks to tell us about something that inspired him, and come back to us later with a picture on his phone of art that he made out of that inspiration. The more we spoke with Robert, the more I came to learn details that suggested he had not had an easy life. He lived in a group home of some kind, was not in communication with any family, and had no source of income to speak of. He was often bored and lonely, which is why when he wasn't creating his art he was walking around the neighborhood, talking the ears off anyone who would stop and listen. I don't know whether he ever experienced homelessness, though it seems likely given the rest of his circumstances.

His most memorable piece of art was the one that he never finished, at least for as long as I knew him. It was a large canvas, at least six feet wide. He described it as his masterpiece in the making: a vision of heaven and hell fading into one another, with all the markings of suffering, pain, and darkness beginning at the bottom and rising into the heavenly. When he showed it to us, though, only the bottom half was complete.

"Is it harder to paint heaven than hell?" I inquired.

"It's impossible. I've never seen heaven, I have no idea what it could be like," he replied. "But hell . . . hell, I know."

In the years I've spent working and advocating with people experiencing homeless, I've witnessed hell on earth. Hell looks like people overdosing in the park, being ticketed for their homelessness so many times that police issue an arrest warrant, having an unattended injury so severe that it's crawling with maggots. Hell is also politicians who order the displacement of encampments to score political points with wealthy constituents, or residents who protest the building of affordable housing or a treatment facility because it brings in "the wrong kinds of people."

Hell is so many of the things I didn't have a chance to highlight in this book, like how our broken foster care system functions as a direct pipeline into homelessness.[10] Hell is when a nonprofit doing essential, life-saving work unironically calls another similar nonprofit its "competition." Hell is when a person works tirelessly to get overtime hours only to be denied a housing voucher because they barely exceeded the maximum income threshold (even though that income is still not nearly enough to afford housing without the voucher).

I hope that in the years since I've known him, Robert has been able to see glimpses of heaven as I have in this work. Heaven has looked like friendships made, birthdays celebrated, games played together, cups of coffee (so many cups of coffee). Heaven has been tears of relief over moving into an apartment, finally securing a prescription to manage blood pressure and relieve constant headaches, or deciding to use drugs more safely. Heaven has been the hundreds of young people who have visited The Center as an immersion experience and made a connection they will never forget, all while learning about homelessness and what they can do to end it. It's everything that draws us together instead of tearing us apart.

I started doing this work with hopes of rescuing folks like Robert from hell on earth and giving them heaven. And to be sure, we should strive to make earth more like it is in heaven—generating affordable housing, mental health services, and substance use treatment centers is a great place to start. People with resources opening their hands, homes, and communities to the vulnerable will always be needed.

The longer I do this work, however, the more convinced I am that heaven is found in the midst of hell; forged by broken and resilient hands determined to not let hell have the final say. Some of the most beautiful people I've met have suffered the greatest pains imaginable; authentic joys emerged amid tragic loss; beauty made among the ashes.

Hell was being with Michael, the Marvel movie-lover I took to get glasses, as he was diagnosed with inoperable, terminal lung cancer. It was hearing him say, "I can't believe I spent the last year avoiding COVID and I ended up with lung cancer." It was the agony of watching him deteriorate quickly over the coming months, in too much pain to go to treatment even while he was desperate to live. Hell was when he didn't make it to Christmas, dying in the hospital just a few hours before I had planned to go see him.

In the midst of it all, we scratched and clawed for pieces of heaven together: bringing him a cup of coffee and sitting with him in the early morning before work; finding a pain medication that gave him brief periods of respite; watching *Shang-Chi* together on my laptop while he worked up the strength to move from his wheelchair to his bed; letting him talk to my son on the phone because he would call me at off hours and my toddler insisted on holding my phone and saying "Hi!" back and forth; watching him watch the trailer for *Spider-Man: No Way Home* as he held back his excitement: "I won't tell you anything, but you're going to love it."

Heaven and hell intersected when I went to the hospital even after they told me he had passed, just to see him one last time.

Each chapter in this book has held this tension: the large, mountain-moving work of systemic change and the here-and-now opportunities to forge relationships that are life-giving, empowering, and promote mutual healing. I believe we are called to both, and that we cannot do one without the other. Homelessness will be ended not because a few politicians have epiphanies and make new policies. It will be because communities, housed and unhoused together, force change because they won't tolerate the status quo any longer.

My hope and fervent prayer is that Christians can be champions of this idea—that homelessness is out of sync with God's ideals, a symptom of our brokenness. I pray that we would be so compelled by our mandate to grace and our love of neighbor that homelessness will no longer be excused as an acceptable reality. I pray that the inherent dignity of our unhoused neighbors, made obvious to us because we are too near not to notice, convicts us to make the necessary changes in ourselves and in our communities to end homelessness.

I pray that grace can lead us all home.

HOMELESSNESS AND HOUSING VOTING GUIDE

I WANT TO make it abundantly clear that homelessness will not be ended by simply voting for the right people or the right measures. Homelessness is a deeply complex issue, the result of bad policies but also of deeply ingrained beliefs and patterns of behavior. My decision to include a voting guide is to supplement, not replace, the work of identifying and renouncing these beliefs.

Nonetheless, policies and politicians have the power to improve or worsen homelessness in the communities where they are installed. Federal policy is significant when it comes to homelessness. Previous administrations have gutted HUD (the federal department of Housing and Urban Development) and stunted the nation's ability to maintain and increase affordable housing and vouchers. At the same time, I find that some of the most immediately impactful legislation and action happens at the smallest, most local levels of government.

City council, county supervisors, school superintendents, judges, and ballot measures have had direct and identifiable effects on homelessness in Los Angeles. These down-ballot contests are usually the least studied and attended to by the average voter. For years I also treated these parts of the ballot as insignificant; marking names according to party alone and making decisions on a cursory glance. After a year of working in direct services, though, I had clearly seen the impact of policies and the power of elected officials to make life better and worse for unhoused communities. I could no longer consider my local elections so indifferently.

Giving more time and attention to local politics has allowed me to see particular patterns and pitfalls. Unfortunately, neither Democrats nor Republicans have the edge on good homelessness policy. Additionally, politicians of all stripes have learned to couch all their policies in the language of compassion, even explicitly using terms like *housing*, but with a variety of different meanings. The discernment of their true intentions is therefore all the more difficult. It's rare to hear a politician come out and say that unhoused people are undesirable and should be removed—yet this is still the default homelessness policy of most elected officials.

While we clearly need to dig a little deeper to find the true intentions and impact of these choices, I don't expect everyone to become an expert on housing and homelessness policy. My goal in this guide, then, is to convey some lessons learned to quickly cut through the surface-level rhetoric to identify the potential impact of a voting outcome. It is not a guarantee, of course—I've seen politicians and policies completely reverse course despite saying *all* the right things and having the full support of allies and advocates. We can scrutinize only what we are given, and it is my experience that most of the time, candidates say enough for us to know what they're after.

Slippery language

The first thing to look for is the way homelessness and unhoused people are talked about. I'm less concerned with terminology—as I stated in the opening of this book, there are reasons for and against the use of *homeless, unhoused,* or *people experiencing homelessness,* and when it comes to policy and politicians, simple word choice is almost never a telltale sign of efficacy or value. Most policies use *homeless* because it is still the predominant terminology, and politicians will use whichever word is favored by their desired voters.

Instead, we need to pay attention to *how* they speak about unhoused people. Fundamentally, if unhoused people reside in a municipality, that makes them constituents. Policies and politicians should speak about them—even to them!—as such. When unhoused people are talked about as if they are not part of the community, this should be an immediate red flag. It's often subtle, but can be found if you look for it: consistent use of "us" and "them" binaries, or perpetuation of the idea that unhoused people come from a different city or neighborhood than yours.

While many politicians—perhaps even especially progressive ones—have learned to be careful when talking about unhoused people, discussions of where and how those people live continues to be a revealing topic. As we discussed in chapter 4, encampments engender *a lot* of animosity. An incredible amount of political time and attention is devoted to eliminating encampments rather than understanding the purpose they serve or the benefits they offer to unhoused people. An agenda based on encampment removal or displacement should always be opposed. Political candidates may talk about reclaiming public spaces like parks or sidewalks, without consideration that unhoused people are part of the public and are using the space for survival.

Keep an eye out for how this is often disguised in language of justice and sympathy. The following are coded ways of promoting anti-camping policy, directly quoted from current elected officials or candidates:

"Street encampments are unsafe, unhealthy, and quite simply —inhumane."[1]

"The streets are no place for our unhoused neighbors to live."[2]

"[Sleeping under a subway stairwell] is not acceptable. That is not dignity. That is disgusting. And that's not who we are as a city."[3]

Notice how each of these appeals to compassion and humanity. At first glance, a compassionate voter would agree with these sentiments. Yet each of them leads to the same conclusion from the same three politicians:

"We must engage every measure available in order to get them off the streets. If that means using the assistance of law enforcement, I support it."[4]

"A person experiencing homelessness should have a clear 'choice date,' after which they are no longer permitted to remain where they have been encamped. And our public parks—essential for everyone's recreation and enjoyment in a park-poor city—should be off-limits to encampments in the first place."[5]

"No more smoking, no more doing drugs, no more sleeping, no more doing barbecues on the subway system. No more just doing whatever you want. No. Those days are over."[6]

Simply diagnosing that sleeping on the streets is a problem is not enough. Even those who pay lip service to the impact of homelessness on the unhoused—as opposed to its impact on businesses or housed people—frequently arrive at the wrong conclusions. People sleep on the streets because there is not a safer, better alternative. If the resources you are offering are better than life on the streets, you don't need to threaten people into choosing them.

"Housing"

After the supervising city councilmember ordered the clearing of Echo Park Lake and the displacement of its hundred or so unhoused residents (see chapter 4), he claimed that most of them had been "housed." When this claim was interrogated, it was revealed that very few had secured permanent housing. The vast majority had been placed in temporary housing and shelters, some of which have since closed.[7]

A key lesson here is to get specific when you hear the word *housing*. Politicians have caught up with the language of advocates and have begun using the word *housing* in broad and slippery ways. In LA, you will rarely hear the word *shelter* anymore—it's now called "bridge housing." Advocates rightly point out that it is most often a "bridge to nowhere," as there continues to be a vast deficit of permanent housing. In many ways, the terminology of "housing" is being co-opted to do more of the same: build facilities that can get people off the streets but are temporary, undignified, and compulsory.

I don't fundamentally oppose the construction of temporary housing. People experiencing homelessness cannot afford to remain on the streets until public opinion is swayed enough to provide permanent housing at the necessary numbers. These types of short-term solutions can be life-saving, especially in geographies with inclement weather, and provide a measured sense of stability and flourishing when done well. However, we should not see them as the solution to homelessness.

Instead, I encourage suspicion when any nonpermanent housing is being considered. What need is being addressed? More pointedly, *whose* need is being addressed? Are unhoused people asking for more or different shelter options, or are we bowing to the requests of those who want to remove unhoused people from "their" space and are seeking a more subtle way of accomplishing it?

While we're on the topic of housing, we ought to remember that homelessness is primarily an issue of housing access and availability. This means that any legislation pertaining to housing affects homelessness, regardless of whether it uses that language or appears to be connected. As housing costs go up, so does homelessness. And because the housing market is treated as an investment opportunity, it attracts not just homebuyers but large corporations—even international ones.

Every piece of housing legislation should be highly scrutinized, and there are always trade-offs. I am less an expert in housing policy than in homelessness, but I will say this much: We need to be willing to risk getting it wrong on housing policy. Whether through zoning changes, rent control, vacancy taxes, restrictions on ownership, or building requirements, something must change, because we cannot maintain the status quo. The cost of housing cannot continue to rise while wages remain stagnant, or homelessness will continue to skyrocket.

For those privileged to benefit from the current arrangement, we are often ignorant of the ramifications. When property

values go up, it is very often at the expense of the housing inse-
cure, who are now further from being able to attain housing
ownership. For those already on the inside, it is hard to imagine
losing money and power for the sake of the marginalized. But
such is the call of Christ, who himself,

> though he was in the form of God,
>> did not regard equality with God
>> as something to be exploited,
> but emptied himself,
>> taking the form of a slave,
>> being born in human likeness.
> (Philippians 2:6–7)

It is in the very nature of Christ to be willing to give up
power and privilege for the sake of others—as followers of this
Jesus, we respond in kind.

Case study: Tiny homes

All these lessons converge on a topic I'm asked about a lot:
tiny homes. Across the United States and Canada, communities are trying creative solutions to economize limited space and
drive down construction costs. Tiny homes can be built quickly
and cheaply, using recycled or low-cost materials such as ship-
ping crates or plastic. Some of these structures are even being
3D printed. As usual, though, the devil is in the details.

When asked whether I support tiny homes, my immediate response is, "Which ones?" Every detail matters here: How
big are they? What amenities do they include? Where are they
located? Are they supervised, and by whom? Are they designed
to be permanent housing, or temporary shelter? What are the

rules, requirements, and qualifications? Every version of tiny homes I've seen answers these questions differently.

What questions would you want answered if you were the one being designated to live in them? When looking for a place to rent, most online apartment finders give you dozens of different criteria to sort your preferences under—neighborhood, price, square footage, amenities—so you can choose from whatever is left after your "deal-breakers." We shouldn't expect that unhoused people don't have their own questions and deal breakers. Ideally, these projects should be built with the direct input of current or formerly unhoused people, especially the ones expected to move in.

In Los Angeles, the latest version of this is "pallet shelters," usually set up in empty, off-the-beaten path parking lots. They comprise a few dozen eight-by-eight-foot aluminum and fiberglass structures (designed for two individuals each). They are supervised by nonprofits, and come complete with a large fence around them guarded by security. The structures look like sheds, and the whole facility looks like a prison camp (though even jail cells are larger). Each time one is built, it is followed by a new ban on street camping at a particular location, and those residents are given "priority placement." As is the case with the "bridge home" facilities, there is still little exit strategy, as unhoused Angelenos wait for permanent housing that doesn't exist at the volume needed. Communities, and their elected officials, get praise for creating an "innovative solution" and for cleaning up the sidewalks. Meanwhile, the unhoused people who moved in (under duress) are worse off, unhoused people who *didn't* get to move in are further criminalized, and what little budget the community has for homeless services is further depleted without creating a sustainable solution.

On the other end of the spectrum are two tiny home projects that I admire: The Village at Glencliff in Nashville, Tennessee, and the Community First! Village in Austin, Texas.

The Village at Glencliff offers transitional housing, but looks nothing like the pallet shelters. They actually look like houses, and come in sizes of two hundred square feet for an individual and four hundred for anyone with a partner or child. The village itself resembles a neighborhood; there is a community garden, a dog park, and open community space. People are offered three meals a day, daily medical checks, and a variety of other services. Residents are allowed to stay until they transition to permanent housing. The village is the brainchild of United Methodist minister Ingrid McIntyre, whose congregation offered a portion of their land to make the project happen.[8]

Community First! Village has similar faith roots, but is a project with a much vaster scope. On fifty-one acres of land sit 120 micro-homes, one hundred RVs, and twenty cottages. It is quite literally a village of its own, with several community-based amenities: outdoor kitchens, a cinema, an organic farm, a market, and more. There are also in-village businesses to provide employment, including a forge, a woodworking shop, a screen printer, and car care. These homes are also designed to be permanent. This is no shelter or transition—it's a home. Like The Village at Glencliff, it prioritizes dignity and flourishing, using tiny homes as an efficient means to uplift people in need—as opposed to trying to relocate people off the street in the cheapest way possible.[9]

All tiny home projects are fascinating in the way they represent both innovation and compromise. Knowing that the state of homelessness is nearly a century in the making and will take a lot of time to resolve, out-of-the-box thinking is sorely needed. At the same time, we must resist the temptation to surrender to the forces in our world that say unhoused people deserve less and should be permanently separate from society.

If we learn to ask the right questions—or listen to the unhoused people who are—we will be able to sift through the rhetoric around proposals like this. We should always be suspicious of a solution to address homelessness that falls short of permanent housing and wraparound care. While we may have to consider some temporary solutions as stopgaps, we need to remain attentive to the quality and dignity of the facilities and who it is they *really* benefit.

Follow the leaders

If this all feels a bit daunting, I have good news: it is more than likely that people or groups in your area are already doing advocacy work you can lean on. Whether it's an especially grounded service provider, a mutual aid group, or a street publication, there are people who pore over every detail of proposed legislation and every platform of every candidate for local government and share their recommendations. Find someone you trust—someone who also has the trust of unhoused people—and take their word for it.

And while you're at it, spend more time with these groups. Join them in doing outreach, advocacy, activism, celebration, and mourning. If homelessness will be ended, it will be because we look beyond the ballot box and live in solidarity. Voting can be a crucial step in generating aid—or preventing additional harm—but the true and holy work happens in the day-to-day communion of neighbors. Follow the lead of your local advocacy and aid groups, to the ballot box and beyond. In doing so, I believe you follow Jesus.

ACKNOWLEDGMENTS

THE FIRST THING that I ever *seriously* wanted to be when I grew up (besides Spider-Man, of course) was a writer. In so many ways, then, to acknowledge everyone who helped make this book possible would require thanking everyone who ever supported and encouraged my writing. Chief among them were my parents, who treated my earliest superhero rip-offs, contrived comic strips, and fan fiction of my favorite television shows like they deserved a Pulitzer. They acted like my writing was great long before it was even good, and I doubt it ever would have been without that.

My primary support in writing *this* book—and for my life altogether—is my wife, Naomi Wilson. She believed in this project before I did; bringing it up regularly over the years, and helping me believe that it needed not only to be written, but to be written by me. Her enthusiasm and excitement has never wavered, even when mine has. Far more valuable than her encouragement, though, has been her gift of time. This book had to be written in the little free time we had between our full-time careers and having our first child, Micah. It was possible only because she *made* time by taking Micah out on adventures every weekend while I stayed behind to write; to say nothing of the lost time with just us in the evenings while I typed away. I am so grateful, and I owe you so many days off from parenting, and date nights galore.

I wish that I could spend pages naming all the current and formerly unhoused people who have shaped my life, my work, and ultimately the content of this book. As a rule, though, I've changed the names of anyone from whom I've not gotten permission to name, so it would do little good to write out hundreds of pseudonyms. Nevertheless, I hope I have done justice to your stories and your truths.

To all the beautiful people I have called my colleagues in this work, I'm so grateful for everything you've taught me and all that you've journeyed through with me. Kelvin, Paige, Nathan, Alex, Douglas, Jocelyn, Stephen, Liz, Devin, and Frank: back when the entire staff could fit in a conference room, you welcomed me in, answered way too many of my questions, and instilled in me the values I still hold closest. Many of you remain my closest friends, confidants, and dialogue partners on these topics.

To Kascha, our first Jesuit Volunteer, who set the gold standard for yearlong service and became a lifelong friend. To the Wellness crew "dream team" who made so many memories together: Paige (again!), Emma, Rome, Garry, Malinda, and Kinsey. To Rudy, who took me under his wing and showed me Los Angeles in a way I'll never forget. To so many others: Elyse, Kate, Chessie, Rachel, Delaney, Richelle, Stephanie, Brian, Herm, Hector, Khady, Sarah, Martha, Josh P., Josh H., Christine, Rochelle, Ladijah, Jackie C., Krys, Nathan B., Adam, Jackie V., Jessica, Annie, Kristian, Araceli, Maria, Damian, Julie, Ana, Melinda. There are so many I've missed.

I'm grateful to Taylor Schumann, who after reading some of the earliest versions of this book decided to recommend me to her agent, Keely Boeving. Keely took a chance on me, and on this book, and I'm forever thankful for the trust and guidance back when I had so little to show for it.

I have immense gratitude for my friend Chase Weaver, who has edited my writing since before this book. If he knew how good he was at it, I could never afford him. (And if this section feels rambly, it's because it never fell under his watchful eye.) Chase has an uncanny ability to challenge my ideas and shine a light on the holes in my arguments and stories—while also putting up with my egregious overuse of cute phrases and my habit of interchanging parentheses, commas, and em dashes as if they all do the same thing.

To Laura, Alyssa, Amy, and the entire team at Herald Press, who have been cheerleaders and collaborators since signing— thank you from the bottom of my heart.

NOTES

Foreword
1   Terence Lester (@imTerenceLester), Twitter, April 20, 2022,
    9:33 a.m., https://twitter.com/imTerenceLester/status/
    1516787201333415942; https://twitter.com/imTerenceLester/
    status/1516787202377895941.

A Note on Language
1   "Can You Guess the Average Age of Homelessness in the United
    States?" *First Focus on Children*, July 27, 2015, https://firstfocus
    .org/blog/can-you-guess-the-average-age-of-homelessness-in-the
    -united-states.
2   Marybeth Shinn and Jill Khadduri, *In the Midst of Plenty: Homeless-
    ness and What To Do About It*, 1st ed. (Hoboken: Wiley-Blackwell,
    2020), 19.

Introduction
1   We will explore in depth how best to understand and thoughtfully
    navigate encounters like this in chapter 3.
2   "UN Rapporteur Compares LA's Skid Row to a Refugee Camp,"
    Chasing the Dream, November 2, 2018, https://www.pbs.org/wnet/
    chasing-the-dream/stories/un-rapporteur-compares-las-skid-row-to
    -a-refugee-camp/.
3   "Distinctive Wesleyan Emphases," United Methodist Church,
    last modified May 31, 2019, https://www.umc.org/en/content/
    distinctive-wesleyan-emphases.
4   "Christians Are More Than Twice as Likely to Blame a Person's
    Poverty on Lack of Effort," *Washington Post*, August 3, 2017, https://
    www.washingtonpost.com/news/acts-of-faith/wp/2017/08/03/
    christians-are-more-than-twice-as-likely-to-blame-a-persons-poverty
    -on-lack-of-effort/.

Chapter 1
1 Gustavo Gutiérrez, *We Drink from Our Own Wells: The Spiritual Journey of a People*, trans. Matthew J. O'Connell, anniv. ed. (Maryknoll, NY: Orbis, 2003), chap. 3.

Chapter 2
1 William Yu, "Homelessness in the U.S., California, and Los Angeles," UCLA Anderson Forecast, June 2018, 7, https://www.anderson.ucla.edu/documents/areas/ctr/forecast/reports/uclaforecast_June2018_Yu.pdf.
2 Some specific exceptions exist. For example, LGBTQ+ youth who are put out of their homes by rejecting parents are likely to leave those neighborhoods for places they assume will be more accepting, like Los Angeles. This cannot account for LA's homelessness rates overall, but it is a significant exception to the rule.
3 Marybeth Shinn and Jill Khadduri, *In the Midst of Plenty: Homelessness and What To Do About It*, 1st ed. (Hoboken: Wiley-Blackwell, 2020), 70.
4 "Congregate shelters" refer to any shelter where beds are all together in a common space, as opposed to shelters that may offer individual or two-person rooms.
5 Stephen Burger, "Arise, Take Up Thy Mat, and Walk," *Policy Review* 79 (September/October 1996), 22.
6 Morgan Lee, "Homelessness Is Vexing American Cities. Do Christians Have a Solution?" *Christianity Today*, May 28, 2021, https://www.christianitytoday.com/ct/podcasts/quick-to-listen/homelessness-cities-poverty-housing-podcast.html.
7 Shinn and Khadduri, *In the Midst of Plenty*, 85.
8 Malcolm Gladwell, "Million Dollar Murray," *New Yorker* 82, no. 1 (February 13, 2006).
9 Shinn and Khadduri, *In the Midst of Plenty*, 85.
10 Deborah Padgett, Benjamin Henwood, and Sam Tsemberis, *Housing First: Ending Homelessness, Transforming Systems, and Changing Lives* (New York: Oxford University Press, 2015), 3.
11 Shinn and Khadduri, *In the Midst of Plenty*, 83.
12 "The Movement," Community Solutions, December 23, 2021, https://community.solutions/built-for-zero/the-movement/.
13 Audrey Jensen, Jill Ryan, Chloe Jones, and Madeline Ackley, "Two Cities Tried to Fix Homelessness, Only One Has Yet Succeeded," *Houston Chronicle*, December 28, 2020, https://www.houstonchronicle.com/news/houston-texas/houston/article/Two-cities-tried-to-fix-homelessness-only-one-15825633.php.
14 Walter Brueggemann, *The Land: Place as Gift, Promise, and Challenge in Biblical Faith*, 2nd ed. (Minneapolis: Fortress Press, 2002), 204.
15 Brueggemann, 205.
16 Los Angeles Homeless Services Authority, "2019 Greater Los Angeles Homeless Count Presentation," updated June 17, 2020, available at

https://www.lahsa.org/documents?id=3437-2019-greater-los-angeles
-homeless-count-presentation.pdf.

17 Matthew Desmond, *Evicted: Poverty and Profit in the American City*,
repr. ed. (New York: Crown, 2017), 303.

18 Eddie S. Glaude Jr., *Democracy in Black: How Race Still Enslaves the
American Soul*, repr. ed. (New York: Crown, 2017), 14–15.

19 "About The Gap: A Shortage of Affordable Rental Homes," National
Low Income Housing Coalition, accessed March 1, 2022, https://
reports.nlihc.org/gap/about; "Canadian Rental Housing Index," Tab-
leau Software, accessed March 1, 2022, http://rentalhousingindex
.ca/en/#comp_fed.

20 Desmond, *Evicted*, 313.

21 "The Gap: A Shortage of Affordable Rental Homes," National Low
Income Housing Coalition, accessed March 1, 2022, https://reports
.nlihc.org/gap/about.

22 Howard Kurtz, "Reagan Budget to Slash Housing Aid," *Washington
Post*, January 30, 1985, https://www.washingtonpost.com/archive/
politics/1985/01/30/reagan-budget-to-slash-housing-aid/f04754a4
-6737-4550-bc4e-df8df0e56e84/.

Chapter 3

1 Los Angeles Homeless Services Authority, "2019 Youth Homelessness Briefing Key Messages," July 31, 2019, available at https://www
.lahsa.org/documents?id=3567-2019-youth-homelessness-briefing
-key-messages.

2 As so many unhoused people are not linked to primary care, emergency departments become the primary way that people experiencing homelessness access medical care. Matt Tinoco, "For Homeless
Californians, the Doctor Is Often the ER—Street Medicine Aims to
Change That," KPBS, December 30, 2019, https://www.kpbs.org/
news/health/2019/09/30/homeless-californians-doctor-often-er
-street-medic.

3 The vibrant communities that unhoused people create, and the ways
in which we often sabotage them, will be addressed thoroughly in
the next chapter.

4 "What Is Trauma?" Trauma-Informed Care Implementation Resource Center, March 20, 2018, https://www.traumainformedcare
.chcs.org/what-is-trauma/.

5 Harry Stack Sullivan, *The Interpersonal Theory of Psychiatry* (New
York: W. W. Norton, 1968).

6 Irvin D. Yalom, *Love's Executioner: And Other Tales of Psycho-
therapy*, 2nd ed. (New York, NY, Basic Books, 2012), 112.

Chapter 4

1 Hannah Bowman, "Encampments for the Unhoused Are Sacred
Structures," *Sojourners*, May 25, 2021, https://sojo.net/articles/
encampments-unhoused-are-sacred-structures.

2 Reporter Rob Eshman thoughtfully connects this festival with the experience of homelessness. Rob Eshman, "For the Homeless, Sukkot Is Year-Round," *The Forward*, October 4, 2020, https://forward.com/news/455781/for-the-homeless-sukkot-is-year-round/.

3 Harking back to our chapter on housing, it was crucial that these new locations were in the same neighborhood as the encampment was previously.

4 Systemic racism (also known as structural or institutional racism) "refers to the complex interactions of large scale societal systems, practices, ideologies, and programs that produce and perpetuate inequities for racial minorities. The key aspect of structural or systematic racism is that these macro-level mechanisms operate independent of the intentions and actions of individuals, so that even if individual racism is not present, the adverse conditions and inequalities for racial minorities will continue to exist." Gilbert C. Gee and Chandra L. Ford, "Structural Racism and Health Inequities," *Du Bois Review: Social Science Research on Race* 8, no. 1 (April 2011): 115–32, https://doi.org/10.1017/S1742058X11000130.

5 Jeffrey Olivet et al., *SPARC: Phase One Findings* (Austin: Center for Social Innovation, 2018), http://center4si.com/wp-content/uploads/2018/03/SPARC-Phase-1-Findings-March-20181.pdf.

6 Ryann Blackshere Vargas, "Glendale Becomes First CA City to Recognize History as Sundown Town," Spectrum News 1, October 9, 2020, https://spectrumnews1.com/ca/la-east/news/2020/10/09/glendale-becomes-first-ca-city-to-recognize-history-as-sundown-town-.

7 Marybeth Shinn and Jill Khadduri, *In the Midst of Plenty: Homelessness and What To Do About It*, 1st ed. (Hoboken: Wiley-Blackwell, 2020), 61.

8 Lauren Hepler, "A Black Couple 'Erased Themselves' from Their Home to See If the Appraised Value Would Go Up. It Did—by Nearly $500,000," *San Francisco Chronicle*, December 3, 2021, https://www.sfchronicle.com/bayarea/article/Black-Marin-City-couple-sues-appraiser-for-16672840.php.

9 Office of Tax Expenditures, "Tax Expenditures," US Department of the Treasury, October 16, 2017, https://www.treasury.gov/resource-center/tax-policy/Documents/Tax-Expenditures-FY2019.pdf; Maggie McCarty, Libby Perl, and Katie Jones, *Overview of Federal Housing Assistance Programs and Policy*, Congressional Research Service, RL34591, updated March 27, 2019, https://crsreports.congress.gov/product/pdf/RL/RL34591. The $148 billion figure accounts only for mortgage interest deductions on owner-occupied homes, property tax deductions on owner-occupied homes, and capital gains deductions on home sales. These are only three of the many deductions and benefits afforded homeowners. Unlike the conservative estimate for homeowner benefits, McCarty, Perl and Jones present a thorough study of all federal programs designed to assist with housing.

10 US Census Bureau, "Historical Census of Housing Tables: Home-ownership by Race and Hispanic Origin," accessed March 3, 2022, https://www.census.gov/data/tables/2000/dec/coh-ownershipbyrace .html.

11 Gale Holland, "Attacked, Abused and Often Forgotten: Women Now Make up 1 in 3 Homeless People in L.A. County," *LA Times*, October 28, 2016, http://www.latimes.com/projects/la-me-homeless -women/.

12 Violence against trans women, especially trans women of color, is at an all-time high. Madeline Carlisle, "Anti-Trans Violence and Rhetoric Reached Record Highs across America in 2021," *Time*, December 30, 2021, https://time.com/6131444/2021-anti-trans-violence/.

13 "Bibliotherapy," *Psychology Today*, accessed March 3, 2022, https://www.psychologytoday.com/us/therapy-types/bibliotherapy.

14 Jeanette Winterson, *Why Be Happy When You Could Be Normal?* (New York: Grove Press, 2013).

Chapter 5

1   "Fast Facts about Mental Health and Mental Illness," CMHA National, July 19, 2021, https://cmha.ca/brochure/fast-facts-about -mental-illness/.

2   "Mental Illness," National Institute of Mental Health, last updated January 2022, https://www.nimh.nih.gov/health/statistics/mental -illness.

3   "Severe Mental Illness," Behavioral Health Evolution, accessed March 3, 2022, https://www.bhevolution.org/public/severe_ mental_illness.page.

4   About one in five Americans and Canadians experience mental illness. "Mental Illness"; "Fast Facts about Mental Health."

5   "Mental Illness."

6   E. Fuller Torrey, *American Psychosis: How the Federal Government Destroyed the Mental Illness Treatment System* (Oxford: Oxford University Press, 2013).

7   If measured by the number of people diagnosed with mental illness, the three largest "mental health facilities" are jails: Twin Towers in Los Angeles, Cook County Jail in Chicago, and Rikers Island in New York City. "The Three Biggest Mental Health Centers in America Are Jails," WLNS 6 News, February 26, 2020, https://www.wlns.com/ news/national/the-three-biggest-mental-health-centers-in-america -are-jails/.

8   "Mental Illness and Homelessness," National Coalition for the Homeless, last modified February 21, 2012, https://www .nationalhomeless.org/factsheets/Mental_Illness.html; "How Many Individuals with Serious Mental Illness Are in Jails and Prisons?" Treatment Advocacy Center, updated November 2014, https://www .treatmentadvocacycenter.org/storage/documents/backgrounders/

how_20many_20individuals_20with_20serious_20mental_
20illness_20are_20in_20jails_20and_20prisons_20final.pdf.

9 "Anosognosia," National Alliance on Mental Illness," accessed
March 28, 2022, https://www.nami.org/About-Mental-Illness/
Common-with-Mental-Illness/Anosognosia.

10 I have omitted the third aspect, "remembrance and mourning," from
this list because it involves the reconstruction of traumatic memory
and mourning the associated loss. This step should only be conducted by a trained therapist.

11 Judith Lewis Herman, *Trauma and Recovery: The Aftermath of
Violence—from Domestic Abuse to Political Terror* (New York: Basic
Books, 2015), 130.

12 Herman, 160.

13 Herman, 196–206.

14 Herman, 214.

Chapter 6

1 Marybeth Shinn and Jill Khadduri, *In the Midst of Plenty: Homelessness and What To Do About It*, 1st ed. (Hoboken: Wiley-Blackwell,
2020), 30.

2 "Substance Abuse and Homelessness," National Coalition for the
Homeless, last modified July 2009, https://www.nationalhomeless
.org/factsheets/addiction.pdf.

3 We will examine this more closely in the next chapter related to
addiction and recovery.

4 "Deaths by Age and Cause—Data Details," *Injury Facts* (blog), last
modified March 24, 2022, https://injuryfacts.nsc.org/all-injuries/
deaths-by-demographics/deaths-by-age/data-details/.

5 "Deaths by Age and Cause."

6 "Recent Trends In Mortality Rates and Causes of Death Among
People Experiencing Homelessness In Los Angeles County" *County
of Los Angeles Public Health,* October 2019, http://publichealth
.lacounty.gov/chie/reports/HomelessMortality_CHIEBrief_Final.pdf.

7 Lindsay Stokes, "Hope for America's Opioid Epidemic Is Grace in a
Syringe," *Christianity Today*, August 15, 2017, https://www
.christianitytoday.com/ct/2017/august-web-only/how-church-can
-save-america-from-opioid-epidemic-fellowship.html.

8 John Bacon, "Ohio Councilman: After 2 Overdoses, No More
EMS," *USA Today*, June 28, 2017, https://www.usatoday.com/story/
news/nation/2017/06/28/ohio-councilman-suggests-three-strikes
-law-halt-overdose-rescues/434920001/.

9 Cleve R. Wootson Jr., "Why This Ohio Sheriff Refuses to Let His
Deputies Carry Narcan to Reverse Overdoses," *Washington Post*,
July 7, 2017, https://www.washingtonpost.com/news/to-your
-health/wp/2017/07/08/an-ohio-countys-deputies-could-reverse
-heroin-overdoses-the-sheriff-wont-let-them/.

10 "Spirit of Harm Reduction: A Toolkit for Communities of Faith Facing Overdose," National Harm Reduction Coalition, January 1, 2021, https://harmreduction.org/issues/harm-reduction-basics/spirit-of-harm-reduction-a-toolkit-for-communities-of-faith-facin-overdose/.

11 It's telling that this story is about a *woman* caught in adultery. We know that adultery requires two participants, yet only one was worthy of death, according to the custom. This should serve as a reminder of our examination of how systems affect communities differently in chapter 4.

12 Maia Szalavitz, *Unbroken Brain: A Revolutionary New Way of Understanding Addiction*, repr. ed. (New York: Picador, 2017), 236–37.

13 Dietrich Bonhoeffer and John W. de Gruchy, *Letters and Papers from Prison*, ed. Victoria J. Barnett (Minneapolis: Fortress Press, 2015).

Chapter 7

1 "Drug Misuse and Addiction," National Institute on Drug Abuse, July 10, 2020, https://nida.nih.gov/publications/drugs-brains-behavior-science-addiction/drug-misuse-addiction.

2 "About Chronic Diseases," Centers for Disease Control and Prevention, April 28, 2021, https://www.cdc.gov/chronicdisease/about/index.htm.

3 William L. White, Christy K. Scott, Michael L. Dennis, and Michael G. Boyle, "It's Time to Stop Kicking People Out of Addiction Treatment," *Counselor* 6, no. 2 (April 2005): 12–25.

4 Maia Szalavitz, *Unbroken Brain: A Revolutionary New Way of Understanding Addiction*, repr. ed. (New York: Picador, 2017), 38.

5 Kara R. Douglas et al., "Adverse Childhood Events as Risk Factors for Substance Dependence: Partial Mediation by Mood and Anxiety Disorders," *Addictive Behaviors* 35, no. 1 (January 2010): 7–13, https://doi.org/10.1016/j.addbeh.2009.07.004.

6 For those in the cycles of addiction, continuing to use these substances also staves off the awful experience of withdrawal. This means that in addition to all the benefits the substances provide, to *not* use means inviting a torrent of incredibly unpleasant symptoms.

7 Edgar Allan Poe to John Allan, April 12, 1833, LTR-036, Edgar Allan Poe Society of Baltimore, "Works—Letters E. A. Poe to S. H. Whitman (November 3, 1848 (?))," https://www.eapoe.org/works/letters/p4811030.htm.

8 Szalavitz, *Unbroken Brain*, 13.

9 "Drug War Statistics," Drug Policy Alliance, accessed March 12, 2022, https://drugpolicy.org/issues/drug-war-statistics.

10 Emily Widra and Tiana Herring, "States of Incarceration: The Global Context 2021," Prison Policy Initiative, September 2021, https://www.prisonpolicy.org/global/2021.html.

11 Steven Belenko, Matthew Hiller, and Leah Hamilton, "Treating Substance Use Disorders in the Criminal Justice System," *Current*

Psychiatry Reports 15, no. 11 (November 2013), https://doi.
org/10.1007/s11920-013-0414-z.

12 The Chicago School, "Any Positive Change," *Insight Digital Magazine*, February 21, 2019, https://www.thechicagoschool.edu/insight/
news/any-positive-change/.

13 Suzanne H. Gage and Harry R. Sumnall, "Rat Park: How a Rat
Paradise Changed the Narrative of Addiction," *Addiction* 114, no. 5
(2019): 917–22, https://doi.org/10.1111/add.14481.

14 Johann Hari, *Chasing the Scream: The First and Last Days of the War
on Drugs* (New York: Bloomsbury, 2015), 293.

Chapter 8

1 Walter Brueggemann, "Enough Is Enough," *The Other Side* 37, no. 5
(November–December 2001).

2 Brueggemann.

3 Chanju Mwanza, "Poverty Porn: Perpetuating Stereotypes and
Denying Real Activism," *VERVE: She Said* (blog), August 16, 2018,
https://medium.com/verve-up/poverty-porn-perpetuating
-stereotypes-and-denying-real-activism-11f682b7d697.

4 Ray B. Browne and Michael T. Marsden, eds., *The Cultures of Celebrations*, 1st edition (Bowling Green, OH: Popular Press 1, 1994).

Conclusion

1 Except for congregate shelters, of course. Large communal settings
have essentially been in and out of quarantine since the pandemic
started.

2 Each city's continuum of care is responsible for submitting homeless
counts to the US Department of Housing and Urban Development
each year, but many were granted exceptions in 2021 because of
COVID, including Los Angeles, since these counting efforts are
often led by volunteers and facilitated in large groups.

3 "Coronavirus Disease 2019," Centers for Disease Control and Prevention, December 21, 2020, https://www.cdc.gov/media/
releases/2020/p1218-overdose-deaths-covid-19.html.

4 From his campaign website: "For those who refuse to go into shelters
or permanent housing, we must engage every measure available in
order to get them off the streets. If that means using the assistance
of law enforcement, I support it." Joe Buscaino, "My Plan for a Safer
L.A.," accessed March 6, 2022, https://www.joebuscaino.com/
a-safer-la.

5 Anthony Macuk, "Wheeler's Office Outlined Plan for a Trio of
1,000-Person Homeless Shelters," KGW, February 4, 2022, https://
www.kgw.com/article/news/local/homeless/portland-mayor-pitched
-1000-person-group-shelters/283-80f54265-0a3b-4af8-85e8
-2c5af5c2b699.

6 See the supplemental voting guide in the appendix to learn more

about how to spot good and bad policy on homelessness in a sea of slippery rhetoric.

7   Alex Hasenstab, "Oregon Coastal City Limits Number of Meals Churches Can Feed Homeless," OPB, October 28, 2021, https://www.opb.org/article/2021/10/28/oregon-coastal-city-limits-free-meals-for-homeless/.

8   Andy Newman, "Feed the Hungry? You'll Need a Permit for That," *New York Times*, December 14, 2021, https://www.nytimes.com/2021/12/14/nyregion/newark-prohibiting-feeding-homeless.html.

9   "Oregon Church Sues after City Says It Can Only Give Out Free Meals Twice a Week to the Homeless," *Washington Post*, accessed March 6, 2022, https://www.washingtonpost.com/nation/2022/02/03/oregon-church-sues-brookings-city/.

10 One out of every four youth who age out of foster care will become unhoused. "Housing and Homelessness," National Foster Youth Institute, May 27, 2021, https://nfyi.org/issues/homelessness/.

Appendix

1   Joe Buscaino, "My Plan for a Safer L.A.," accessed March 6, 2022, https://www.joebuscaino.com/a-safer-la.

2   Mike Feuer, "Homelessness," accessed March 13, 2022, https://www.mikeforla.com/homelessness.

3   Note how the *New York Post* article quoting this speech uses obvious othering language: Editorial board, "Eric Adams' Homeless Plan Is Safer for Us and Better for Them," *New York Post*, February 21, 2022, https://nypost.com/2022/02/21/eric-adams-homeless-plan-is-safer-for-us-and-better-for-them/.

4   Buscaino, "My Plan for a Safer L.A."

5   Feuer, "Homelessness."

6   Editorial board, "Eric Adams' Homeless Plan."

7   KABC, "Despite Chaos, Councilman O'Farrell Calls Clearing of Echo Park Homeless Encampment a Success as Repair, Renovation Project Proceeds," ABC7 Los Angeles, March 28, 2021, https://abc7.com/echo-park-lake-homeless-encampment-los-angeles-lapd/10454487/.

8   "About," The Village at Glencliff, accessed March 13, 2022, https://www.villageatglencliff.org/about.

9   "Community First! Village," Mobile Loaves and Fishes, September 9, 2021, https://mlf.org/community-first/.

THE AUTHOR

KEVIN NYE is a homeless services worker and advocate living in Los Angeles with his wife Naomi and son Micah. He has a master of divinity from Fuller Seminary and was formerly a licensed minister in the Church of the Nazarene. With his combined theological education and experience working with the unhoused, Kevin writes about the lives and experiences of the marginalized with urgency and graciousness, inviting and challenging the church to mobilize to end homelessness. You can follow Kevin's work at KevinMNye.com.